The Princeton Review

Mythology
Smart
Junior

A Journey to the Land
of Legend

The Princeton Review

Mythology Smart Junior

A Journey to the Land
of Legend

by Gary Arms, Ph.D.

Random House, Inc., New York 1997

Princeton Review Publishing, L.L.C.
2315 Broadway
New York, NY   10024
E-mail: web-info@review.com

ISBN 0-679-78375-X

Editor: Amy Zavatto
Production Editor: Amy Bryant
Designer: Illeny Maaza
Production Coordinator: Matthew Reilly

Manufactured in the United States of America on recycled paper.

9 8 7 6 5 4 3 2 1

ACKNOWLEDGMENTS

I would like to thank Evan Schnittman for asking me to write this book. I'd like to thank all the Princeton Review staff who worked on this book: Nicole DuCharme, Carrie Smith, John Bergdahl, Greta Englert, Adam Hurwitz, Evelin Sanchez-O'hara, Christopher Thomas, and especially Maria Russo. Most importantly, I'd like to thank Homer, Ovid, and Robert Graves.

Contents

Chapter 1
End Winter Forever!

It was the middle of winter, and Bridget was tired of it. She was tired of snow and cold and ice, tired of wearing layers of clothes, tired of boots and gloves and scarves. Beauregard, an enormous but rather distinguished-looking cat, did not seem to mind the winter, but only because he never ventured outside. He dozed in an armchair parked close to a heat vent and dreamed of a female cat he had once met in the south of France. "Ah, Mimi," he murmured.

"I hate winter," Bridget sighed to herself. "I don't see the point of winter at all!" She opened a pack of bubble gum and stuck two pieces into her mouth. Bridget was fond of bubble gum. She adjusted her Yankees baseball cap.

Knock! Knock! Knock! Knock!

Ding dong!

Glad for some company, Bridget leapt up to open the door. Beauregard opened one eye a slit, to see who had come to call. He rolled over on his back and lazily waved a paw in the air, as if he already knew who it was. Beauregard was an extremely intelligent cat.

Ding dong!

"For pete's sake, I'm coming," Bridget said and threw open the door. There on the other side of it were two kids so hidden in coats, scarves, and hats, it was impossible to be sure who they were.

"Bridget, can we come in?" said one of the bundles of clothes. "Please?"

"Babette?" gasped Bridget. "Is that you?"

"And this is Barnaby!" said Babette.

"Beauregard!" yelled Bridget to the enormous cat. "It's Babette and Barnaby! Wake up!"

Beauregard opened one eye. Oh, no, he thought. Whenever these three kids got together, it always meant trouble. He would definitely have to keep an eye on them.

"Hello, Barnaby," he said. Beauregard prided himself on his excellent manners. The cat extended a glossy black paw in Babette's direction. "Bonjour, Babette."

"It's awfully cold out there!" said Barnaby, pulling off his stocking cap. "We about froze!" His great bushy shock of hair emerged all at once. Full of static electricity, it stood straight up. "Never is it so cold in Paris!" said Babette, who came from the capital of France.

"Oh, I know! I hate winter!" said Bridget. "I can't wait for spring to get here!" She chewed vigorously on her gum.

Barnaby's glasses, which were big and round and made him look a little like an owl, began to steam up. He took them off and cleaned them with the end of his scarf.

"It's so cold here in New York City," said Babette. "Don't you wish we were somewhere warm—like the south of France?"

"Like Hawaii!" shouted Bridget. And she said aloud, "I hate winter. I don't see the point of it at all!"

"I don't know if winter has a point," said Barnaby. He pulled off his scarf and his thick parka. "But I can explain why we have winter." Barnaby was a scientific genius and very fond of explaining things.

"Oh, for pete's sake!" said Bridget, who sometimes got a little tired of Barnaby's explanations, "We all know why there's winter. Because it gets cold!"

"But do you know why it gets cold?" asked Barnaby. Once he started an explanation, it was very hard to stop him.

"Who cares why! It just does!"

"It has to do with earth's orbit around the sun." Barnaby put on his now clean glasses. "The earth's orbit isn't a perfect circle but an ellipsis, an oval. Also, the earth is sort of tilted. So, sometimes, as the earth makes its orbit around the sun, it tilts away from the sun. That's why there's winter."

"Who cares?" said Bridget. She was not in a good mood at all.

"There is another explanation," Babette said. She had removed her stylish black trench coat and put on her retro sunglasses. Babette was very chic. She wore slender black boots and a short black skirt. In fact, all her clothes were black.

"What other explanation?" demanded Barnaby.

"The reason we have winter is because of Persephone." Babette said the strange name slowly: Pur-SEF-uh-nee. "I learned about it in school."

"Who in the world is Perseph—? What'd you call him?" Barnaby frowned suspiciously. "Is he a scientist? I've never heard of him."

"Persephone," repeated Babette. She sat down on the armchair beside Beauregard and stroked the cat's head. "And Persephone isn't a 'he.' She certainly isn't a scientist either."

"I think I've heard this story," said Bridget. "Isn't it a Greek myth or something?" She sat on the floor at Babette's feet.

"A myth!" exclaimed Barnaby. As a scientist, he did had little faith in old myths. "Myths are silly."

"Myths are not at all silly," said Babette. "They are stories, wonderful stories."

"I find them silly and out of date," said Barnaby stubbornly.

"They are certainly ancient," laughed Babette. "No one knows who made them up."

"I like those kind of stories," said Bridget. She sometimes felt Barnaby got too full of himself. As a result, she liked to take Babette's side when her friend argued with him.

"Myths explain some belief —like a religious belief," Babette continued, "or a natural phenomenon. For example, why there are tornadoes or why winter exists."

"I know why there are tornadoes," said Barnaby. "And it has nothing to do with gods and goddesses. It's all because of moisture, air pressure, wind conditions, things like that."

"Barnaby, will you shut up?" said Bridget. "If Babette is going to tell us a story, I want to hear it."

Barnaby sprawled full length on the sofa. Babette was an excellent storyteller. And, though Barnaby thought science the best of all subjects, he was no more immune to a good story than most people.

"If you like," said Babette, tickling Beauregard under the chin in the place he liked best, "I will tell you the story of Persephone, or how we came to have winter."

"Well, go ahead," agreed Barnaby, "just don't try to pretend it's a true story."

"Once upon a time," said Babette, "a most beautiful girl named Persephone lived with her mother, Demeter." She pronounced it "Dih-MEE-tur."

"Oh, these weird names!" complained Barnaby. "Why couldn't she just call her mother 'Mom,' like everybody else?"

"Because Demeter was a goddess."

"That's right," agreed Bridget. "You can't go around calling a goddess 'Mom.' It sounds weird. Even if she is your mother."

"Demeter was one of the most famous and important of the goddesses. She was in charge of all plants. Trees, grasses, flowers, vines, toadstools, everything. One day, Persephone was playing in a field with her friends. All of a sudden, they heard a rumbling noise—like thunder. Except that instead of coming from the sky, it seemed to be coming up from out of the ground."

"An earthquake?" guessed Barnaby. "There must be a fault line running through Greece."

"It was not an ordinary earthquake, but the earth did split open. The girls screamed and fell to their knees. A huge hole opened in the earth, big as a sinkhole. From out of it came a team of black horses. Their manes flickered like black flames and their eyes were red."

"Red?" Barnaby looked doubtful. "You must mean brown."

"Red as fire," insisted Babette. "And their teeth were sharp as shark's teeth."

"But horses eat grass, hay, stuff like that—oats—they don't need sharp teeth."

"Shut up, Barnaby!" said Bridget. "Let her tell the story!"

"The girls screamed at the sight of the terrible horses. Except Persephone. As the daughter of a goddess, she did not show a bit of fear. The horses pulled a chariot. It too was black, just as black as the horses. And in the chariot was a huge warrior, dressed all in black."

"Was he handsome?" asked Bridget.

"Oh, yes, certainly. Very handsome. But he did not smile. While Persephone's friends screamed, the giant warrior leapt out of his chariot. He grabbed Persephone and pulled her back in with him."

"How terrible! Kidnapping!" said Barnaby.

"How exciting!" said Bridget. "Who was he?"

"The warrior whipped the horses. The chariot wheeled around and dropped down into the huge black hole. The earth closed. That was the last anyone saw of them."

"What happened?" said Bridget. "I'll bet Demeter was mad!"

"The goddess was furious. She was so angry, she cursed the world.

"Demeter ordered that never again would any plant grow anywhere in the world, not until her daughter was returned unharmed."

"But all life depends on plants," said Barnaby. "Why, without plants, eventually the whole world would die."

"That is nearly what happened," agreed Babette. "All of the plants turned brown. Their leaves shriveled and fell off. The animals that fed on plants began to starve. If Demeter had not found out what happened to Persephone, the whole world of living things would have died."

"I think I'm beginning to remember it," said Bridget. "The giant warrior—wasn't he the god of the Underworld? I can't remember his name."

"Hades," said Babette. She pronounced the word carefully, "HAY-dees."

"Also known as Pluto!" said Bridget. "That's another thing I remember. The Greeks called the god of the Underworld Hades, but the Romans called him Pluto—like Mickey Mouse's dog!"

"These crazy names!" sighed Barnaby. "Of course, I have heard some of them before. Many of the constellations and planets are named after Greek gods."

Babette smiled. "The most important god of them all was named Zeus. When he saw all the world dying, it made him angry. He ordered Hades to give up Persephone. Hades would have to let the girl return to her mother so that all the plants would start to grow again."

"Did he give her up?" asked Barnaby. "Hades or Pluto or whatever you call him. Did he let her go?"

"Yes, he did. Since Zeus ordered it, he had to. But, on her way out of the underworld, Persephone grew very hungry. She had not eaten or drank anything the whole time she was in the underworld. Persephone stopped beside a pomegranate tree. Do you know what that is, Barnaby?"

"Sure!" yelled Barnaby, offended that anyone would think he did not know the name of a fruit that could be bought in the supermarket. "It's a round, red fruit."

"Inside the pomegranate was a circle of twelve seeds. Persephone ate one of them. She hadn't eaten in so long, it was delicious. She ate another seed and another, six in all."

"I don't see what difference it makes that she ate some seeds," said Barnaby. "What's the big deal?"

"Persephone went back to her mother. Demeter was so overjoyed to have her daughter back that she commanded all the plants to come to life again. The leaves turned green, the vines grew, flowers bloomed."

"But what about those six pomegranate seeds?" demanded Barnaby. He did prefer science, but he liked stories enough to know that if a story tells about someone eating something unusual, it will probably turn out to be important.

"I was just getting to that," Babette said. "Because she had eaten the food of the underworld, Persephone was doomed to stay there forever."

"Forever? Just because she ate some seeds?!"

"Yes, that was the rule. If Persephone ate anything in the underworld, she had to remain there. It was a terrible problem for Zeus, the father of all the gods and goddesses. Because Persephone had eaten the fruit of the underworld, she was doomed to live with Hades. But if she did live with him, Demeter would curse the world again, and everything would die."

"Were all these gods and goddesses hot heads?" asked Barnaby. "Why couldn't they compromise or something?"

"That's exactly what they did. Zeus ruled that since Persephone had eaten the pomegranate seeds, she would have to live in the underworld with Hades. But because she ate only six of the twelve seeds, she would have to live with Hades only six months of the year. The other half-year, she could live with her mother, Demeter."

"And that's why we have winter!" exclaimed Bridget.

"Well, I don't get it," grumbled Barnaby. "Just because she ate some seeds?"

"Sometimes you're such a dope," said Bridget, who loved to prove it when she knew things that Barnaby didn't. "See, what happens is, every year, when Persephone has to go off with Hades and live in the underworld, that's when the leaves turn color and fall off the trees. Everything stops growing. It gets cold and the snow flies. Like now!" She looked out the window of the apartment, or would have looked out if that window had not been covered with frost. "Then, when Persephone gets to come back to her mother and everything starts to grow, that's when spring starts! Now, do you get it?"

"Hmm," said Barnaby, looking very thoughtful.

Bridget said, "I wish we could go back there somehow and save Persephone. Think of it! If only there was a way to save her from Hades, there never would be winter—and I hate winter!"

"Do you know," Barnaby said, "it might be interesting as a science experiment. What would the world be like with out winter?"

Beauregard stood up. "I have an idea," he announced. He wriggled his whiskers.

"Oh-oh!" said Bridget. "Now, we're in trouble." She pointed at Barnaby, who seemed lost in a dream. "He's thinking. You know what that means!"

"Only one person in the world could possibly help us on an adventure like this one." Beauregard smiled his most knowing cat smile. "Merlin Ozymandias."

"Who?" said Babette.

"Also known as Cue Ball."

"What kind of name is that?" demanded Bridget.

"I bet he's bald," said Barnaby.

"Merlin Ozymandias is bald as a billiard ball. Hence, the nickname. He is a world-class expert in mythology and magic."

"Where does he teach?" asked Barnaby. "NYU?"

Beauregard yawned, "Don't be silly. Merlin would never do anything so respectable. Cue Ball Ozymandias goes his own way."

"He sounds like my kind of guy," said Bridget.

"Unfortunately, Cue Ball is not a helpful person. To help us, he will want something. In fact, he will want a lot."

"What? We aren't rich, you know."

"Although Cue Ball sells magic devices, antiques, curios of all kinds, he has one real passion—baseballs."

"Baseball cards, you mean?" asked Bridget. She had quite a collection of her own.

"Oh, no. Cue Ball won't touch baseball cards. He considers them childish. Cue Ball deals exclusively in baseballs. Well, 'deals' is perhaps the wrong word. He doesn't sell baseballs.

Never! He buys them. Cue Ball has a huge collection kept in a vault at his place of business."

"Just baseballs? Any kind of baseballs?" Bridget looked suspicious.

"He collects major league baseballs used in real games. They must be baseballs that have been hit by genuine major leaguers"—Beauregard looked meaningfully at Bridget—"especially Yankees. He's fanatical about the Yankees."

Bridget lowered her eyebrows. "Now, wait just a minute—"

"Let Beauregard finish, Bridget," said Barnaby. "This sounds fascinating."

"Cue Ball's craving for homerun balls is insatiable. I would say, if someone owned such a ball—a homerun ball hit by Reggie Jackson, for example . . ."

"No!" yelled Bridget. "No way, José! That ball is my most valuable possession! Are you kidding? Get outta here!"

But by then, all the others were circling around her. Poor Bridget did not have a chance.

Chapter 2
Don't Call Me "Cue Ball"!

It was a crazy idea. They were going to return to the Land of Myth, save Persephone from Hades, and end winter forever! But Bridget liked crazy ideas. That was why she let the others talk her into giving up her favorite treasure, her Reggie Jackson home run ball. Now that they were standing on the sidewalk outside the store belonging to Merlin "Cue Ball" Ozymandias, Bridget felt mournful when she looked at her ball. Besides, who knew if this weird Cue Ball guy would really be able to help them? Bridget gave her baseball a squeeze and breathed a heavy sigh.

On the store's dirty front window was written:

MAGIC—CURIOS—BASEBALLS

MERLIN OZYMANDIAS, PROPRIETOR

PLEASE ENTER

Barnaby turned the doorknob and pushed open the door, causing a bell to ring.

The door creaked as it opened. Barnaby entered. Babette followed. Beauregard pushed past Bridget and disappeared into the store's interior.

Bridget gazed at her baseball one more time. Then she pushed open the door and entered a room that was long, narrow, and gloomy. It was filled with shelves. All sorts of items were stacked upon these shelves—odd and curious things.

"Merlin?" called Beauregard. He turned to the others and whispered, "Never call him Cue Ball." He strolled further into the shop. "Are you here?"

Behind a counter at one side of the store, a man stood up. "Who's there? Who is it? Whadda yuh want?" It was hard to believe the man could be, as Beauregard claimed, a world-class expert on anything, let alone magic and mythology. He was indeed bald as a cue ball. His fat stomach pushed out the front of his horizontally striped tee shirt. He came around the edge of the counter and walked rapidly toward them, frowning at them suspiciously as if he suspected they might steal something.

"Merlin, how nice to see you after all these years," said Beauregard. "Let me introduce my friends, Bridget, Barnaby, and Babette."

The man looked at the kids; he looked at Beauregard. "Whadda yuh want?"

"A favor, my dear fellow."

"Huh? What kinda favor?"

"A large favor, one only you could perform. We'd like to enter your back room, Merlin. There is something there, a certain cabinet . . ."

"Oh, no, you don't. Not a chance. I never let anyone into that room. Especially not you."

"Bridget," said Beauregard, "show Merlin your treasure."

"What treasure?" said Merlin. His eyes squinted and his thick eyebrows descended suspiciously. The bald top of his head glowed with perspiration.

Reluctantly, Bridget held out her baseball.

At once, Merlin's eyebrows began to jiggle up and down like nervous caterpillars.

"It is a major league baseball," said Beauregard.

"Let me see it!" Merlin's hand leapt out to take the baseball, but Bridget whisked it behind her back again.

"A ball hit out of the park."

"Home run ball?" Merlin bit his lip, trying to conceal his excitement.

"Not just any park. Yankee Stadium. Bridget, tell Merlin the name of the player who hit it out of the park."

Slowly, Bridget brought out the ball again. She turned it until the signature scrawled between its seams came into sight.

"Reggie Jackson!" said Cue Ball in a choked voice. "What do I gotta to do to get it?" He licked his lips.

"As I indicated," Beauregard said, "we desire entry into the back room, the secret room. We would like to see the cabinet. I think you know the one I have in mind."

"Oh, no. Not a chance," Cue Ball said again.

"What a pity. Bridget, you'd better put away that baseball. Well, Merlin, it was nice to see you. Let's go, kids."

They headed toward the door.

"No!" yelled Cue Ball. "Wait."

They stopped.

"I ain't sure it works, Beauregard. And I ain't gonna be held responsible."

"Don't concern yourself, Merlin. This way, kids." Beauregard led the way to the back of the store. "The cabinet that Merlin has hidden in his back room," he told the kids, "is a very, very special cabinet, a magical cabinet carved, or so it is believed, by Hephaestus himself."

"Who?" Bridget said. "Heph who?"

"Huh-FES-tuhs," said Beauregard slowly and purposefully.

They stopped before a large painting of a man shooting an arrow into an enormous snake.

"Do you recognize that scene, Babette?" Beauregard asked.

"No. Is it something from Greek mythology?"

"It is the god Apollo, shooting the Python. Open the door, Merlin."

"Then I get the home run ball? That's the deal? I let you and these kids try out the Cabinet of Hephaestus, and I get the ball?"

"That's right, Merlin. Open up, if you please."

"I want her word too. The owner."

"Bridget?" Beauregard turned to her.

"Go on, Bridget," said Barnaby.

"What if it doesn't work? What if we try out this magic cabinet carved by Heph Whoever-you-said, and nothing happens? Do I still have to give up my ball?"

"In every truly interesting bargain," said Beauregard, "one must take a risk."

Bridget looked mournfully at her baseball.

"That's the deal," said Cue Ball. "I get the ball, or none of you even see the back room."

"I'll give it up—" Bridget said softly.

"Here, give it to me!" Cue Ball's eyebrows jumped up and down like Mexican jumping beans. "Let me see it!"

"—when we try out the cabinet," Bridget said firmly, "and not one second before."

Muttering bitterly to himself, Cue Ball touched a hidden button that caused the painting of Apollo and the Python to vanish into the ceiling.

Behind it was a door. Merlin pulled a huge ring of keys from his pocket, flipped through them until he found the right one, and used it to unlock the door. Once open, the door did not reveal a room. Behind it was another door, made of metal, with a combination lock.

"Turn your backs, all of you!" ordered Merlin. "No peeking!"

They did as he said. They could hear the slight clicks of the tumblers falling as Merlin twirled the dial.

"Okay, let's go," he said. "Don't break nothing."

They followed Cue Ball into a room that was nearly as long as the shop itself. It too was full of shelves, but the objects atop these shelves were carefully displayed. Here, there was no clutter.

"What are all these things?" asked Babette. The shelves were full of fascinating objects.

Bridget kept a firm grip on the baseball.

"This way," said Cue Ball. He led them to the back of the room where something large and rectangular was shrouded by a sheet.

"Remove the sheet, Barnaby," said Beauregard.

Barnaby drew away the sheet, revealing a splendid, hand-carved cabinet. It was as large and roomy as a couple of telephone booths. Its sides were covered with elaborate carvings.

"The Cabinet of who?" said Bridget.

"Huh-FES-tuhs," Beauregard said the name once more, carefully and respectfully. "He was one of them, you see. Their foremost craftsman. When he made a thing, well, you see, it stayed made."

"One of them?" demanded Bridget. "One of who?"

"One of the gods of ancient Greece," said Babette. She had turned a little pale. "I never thought they existed. Not really. Hephaestus. The Romans called him Vulcan. He was the son of Zeus and the husband of Aphrodite, I think."

"One thing I don't get," said Bridget, "is why the gods have two names."

"They don't have two names," snapped Cue Ball.

They looked at him in surprise.

"Their real names are the ancient Greek names. But the Greeks did not conquer the world. Not by arms anyway. The Romans did. They produced the greatest armies and generals ever known in their world. But they were not so creative as the ancient Greeks. They stole their ideas, their art, their medicine, and even their gods. Of course, they changed the names. As she said, the Romans called him Vulcan. But his real name is Hephaestus."

"Quite a speech, Merlin," murmured Beauregard.

The other three exchanged looks, wondering if it could really be true. Was this weird man in fact a world class expert on magic and mythology? He seemed crude. He spoke like someone who could barely read. Yet, there was something about him. Here, in his secret room, surrounded by the ancient treasures he had collected, Merlin Ozymandias seemed to take on dignity. He stood straight. His eyes gleamed.

"Like I said, I ain't never tested it," said Merlin. "Go on, Beauregard. You wanna be first?" He smiled crookedly.

The cat sniffed at one of the figures that was carved on the cabinet door. It was of an amazingly muscular man, a warrior of some sort. He was wearing a lion skin and carrying a huge club.

"We can't very well let one of these kids test it, can we?" said Merlin. "You ain't scared?"

Beauregard stood up on his hind legs. He really was a huge cat. He looked Cue Ball in the eye and said, "Okay, let's go!" Then he turned around, stuck his tail straight up into the air like an exclamation point, and strolled right into the cabinet.

"We'll send him back, all the way to the Land of Myth," said Merlin. "But only for one minute. We don't want him to get into trouble. Even a smart cat like Beauregard can get into trouble in a place like that. Never been there myself, but from what I hear . . . We'll send him back for sixty seconds, then bring him right back."

"I don't think this is a good idea." Bridget chewed vigorously on her gum. "Couldn't we send a mouse back, or a hamster or something?" Beauregard was one of her very best friends. "Or a rat. I don't even like rats!" But the others were so intent on watching what Cue Ball was doing that they did not listen to her.

The bald man closed the door of the cabinet. He tapped the muscular figure the cat had sniffed before entering the cabinet. "Hey, it's warm to the touch," he murmured.

"Beauregard, you all right?" cried Bridget.

The cabinet began to vibrate.

"What's wrong?" yelled Bridget.

The cabinet began to move. In complete and eerie silence, the enormous wooden box rocked back and forth. It moved out from the wall one inch, two inches, then retreated, then ceased to move at all.

"Beauregard!" yelled Bridget. "Open the door!"

There was a loud bang. Then all the lights went out. They were plunged into complete darkness.

"What is it?!" yelled Bridget. "What happened to the lights?"

"I'll get a flashlight," called Cue Ball. "No one move."

The kids froze where they were and waited for Merlin to locate a flashlight. "It's that loud noise I'm worried about," Bridget said nervously. "Beauregard's in there, isn't he?"

"Ouch!" yelled Cue Ball as he tripped over something in the darkness.

At that moment, the lights came back on.

"Are you all right?" Barnaby yelled. "Beauregard!"

"Go on and open the door now," Cue Ball said. "The minute's up."

Barnaby opened the door to the cabinet.

"Beauregard?" said Bridget. "Come out!"

Nothing happened. They all exchanged glances.

"Beauregard?"

They peered into the cabinet. It was empty. There was nothing inside it, not so much as a single whisker.

"I'm going after him!" yelled Bridget.

"Not till you give up that home run ball, you ain't." Cue Ball stood in front of the cabinet, blocking the way and grinning strangely. "You want in there, you give up that ball. That's the deal."

Bridget frowned but did not say a word. She slapped the ball into his hand. "Now, get out of my way." She marched over to the cabinet and went inside. "It's like a little cave in here and it smells funny—like mud, like a swamp or something! Hey!" The door closed behind her.

The cabinet moved. It hopped and jumped, then became still. Bang!

Cue Ball paid no attention. He feasted his eyes on the baseball.

Babette pulled open the cabinet door. "She's gone! Bridget!"

"I can't believe it!" yelled Barnaby. "First Beauregard, then Bridget. Where are they, Cue Ball?"

The bald man looked up, his face flushed with anger. "What'd you call me, kid?"

Barnaby and Babette looked at each other. Cue Ball moved menacingly in their direction.

"Come on, Barnaby!" said Babette. "Come on!" The two kids ran into the Cabinet of Hephaestus. The door slammed shut behind them, and they were plunged into complete darkness.

"Hey!" said Babette. "It does smell like a swamp in here!"

Then the cabinet began to move.

"Oh, no!" yelled Barnaby.

Bang!

Chapter 3
The Swamp

"Where are we?" said Bridget. She was a little dazed. They were definitely no longer in New York. "What is this? Ick!" Like the others, she was standing in knee-deep water.

"It must be some kind of swamp," said Beauregard. Mist rose up all around them. It was hard to see very far in any direction.

"Where's Merlin Ozymandias?" asked Babette. "Where's the Cabinet of Hephaestus?" She began to wade to a dry spot. "It is a good thing I'm wearing my boots."

They were standing in a swamp. The air stank. It smelled of dead fish and mud. "You know what it smells like?" said Bridget. "Dead crab!"

"Is it possible?" asked Barnaby. "Can we be in the Land of Myth?" Barnaby began to say something else, but the words seemed to get trapped in his throat. He gasped. His face turned red, and he pointed up. He did not need to point because the others had already seen it. None of them moved or made a sound. They were afraid to.

If someone had drawn a line from the end of Barnaby's pointing finger, that line would have eventually connected with an enormous reptilian head and a pair of fiery red eyes.

It was a dinosaur of some sort, that was their first thought. The monster was taller than a tree. The snakelike head rose up over the topmost branches of a tall oak. The head looked north, south. The creature's mouth was full of sharp teeth. Even from this distance, they could see those teeth. "Wow!" whispered Bridget. Then something astounding happened.

A second head, identical to the first, rose above the tree. Could there be two monsters? There was something peculiar about the heads. Not only were they identical, but they moved in unison. They nearly touched but did not react to each other.

None of the kids wanted to say it aloud, but Barnaby, Babette, and Bridget all had the same thought. The monster taller than a tree had two heads!

The pair of heads tilted. One looked east out of its bright eyes; the other head looked west.

None of the kids moved. Even Beauregard seemed frightened. They were spellbound. Did the two-headed monster see them? They hardly dared to breathe.

Then another astounding thing happened. As the monster moved closer to them, a third head appeared. The monster had three heads! Each was identical, and terrifying!

The monster began to move away from the tree and away from them. Despite its size, the monster moved gracefully and made very little sound.

"Look," murmured Bridget; she could not help herself.

The monster had two, three, four—they counted them—nine heads!

"I know what it is," said Babette.

The monster moved farther away from them. Its huge body dropped into the swamp. As it swam in the muddy water, its long body swerved from side to side making s-shapes.

The nine snake heads were clearly visible, arching above the water. At last, the mist swallowed up the monster. Not until then did they feel safe enough to talk freely.

"At least I think I know what it is," said Babette. "It is the Hydra."

"I agree," said Beauregard, "and this must be one of the Swamps of Lerna."

Barnaby gave his bushy head of hair a furious shake, and something fell out. A book.

"I knew I brought this along!" Barnaby snatched up the small book. "I just couldn't remember where I put it." The book's title was *A Pocket Guide to Greek Mythology*. Barnaby began to flip through its pages. He found the index in the back and looked up *Hydra*.

"It says, 'See Heracles, Twelve Labors of,'" he told the others. He found the passage about Heracles and skimmed it rapidly. "It says Heracles, pronounced HAIR-uh-kleez, is also known as Hercules. You know, the strongest guy in the world. He had to perform Twelve Labors so that he could become immortal. Let's see. Yeah, it looks like he's up to Labor number two—he has to kill the Lernean Hydra. Hmm." He looked closer at the page. "It says he had an assistant, a boy named—this is a strange one—Iolaus. That's EE-oh-luhs."

They heard a loud gasp.

They turned to look at a nearby bush. There was no breeze, but the bush was trembling. Then it sneezed!

"Oh, oh, oh. Achoo! Achoo!"

"That bush has sneezed twice!" said Babette.

"Well, I'm checking it out," said Bridget. She ran over to the bush and pushed back its branches.

"It's a boy!"

A boy wearing nothing but a sort of smock was crouched on the ground beneath the bush. Obviously, he had been hiding from them.

"Oh, please, holy ones, do not kill me! Please do not turn me into a cow or a goose. Please, I beg you. If you must transform me into something, could I be a horse or even a dog? Anything but a goose!"

"Slow down, kid," said Bridget. "We won't hurt you." She looked at the others and silently mouthed the word, "Crazy."

"I know you must be gods," whispered the boy. He kept his eyes trained on the ground as if he was afraid to look at them. "I saw your talking cat appear out of thin air. Then the two goddesses appeared and the young god. Please, I beg you, I did not mean to look upon you. Spare me!"

"But we are not gods," said Babette.

"Take it easy, kid." Bridget bent down and patted his quivering shoulder. "We're just normal people."

"But, but I heard you speaking of the Hydra and Heracles, my master. You even said my name, Iolaus. If you are not gods, you must belong to them. Are you oracles? Do you tell the future?"

Barnaby moved forward and helped Iolaus to his feet. "Babette and Bridget are telling the truth. We aren't gods and we won't harm you. We're—well, it's kind of hard to explain. But we definitely aren't dangerous."

Babette said, "Iolaus, perhaps you can help us. We have come here to help a girl named Persephone. Do you know where she lives? We want to find her. We have something very important to tell her."

"Yeah," agreed Bridget, "we have to warn Persephone about something. Does she live around here?"

"I don't know. Perhaps my master Heracles does. But I think it unlikely she lives here in the Swamps of Lerna. No one lives here. Anyone who ventures here is never seen again. I am only here because my master must fight the Hydra."

Suddenly, the air was filled with the sound of hideous howling. It was like the blast of a dozen air-raid sirens.

"The Hydra!" gasped Iolaus. "It has begun!"

"What's begun?" demanded Barnaby.

"The battle! My master has attacked the Hydra!"

They climbed a tree to watch. A tall spire of rock rose up from the swamp. A man stood halfway up the spire. Heracles! He was amazingly muscular. It was impossible to see him and not think of Arnold Schwarzenegger. The splendid man wore the skin of a lion draped over his shoulder. He wore a sword at his waist and wielded a huge club.

The Hydra surged toward Heracles, but it lost its footing in the pile of boulders at the foot of the spire.

"Look where Heracles has chosen to stand," said Barnaby. "He is in a cleft of the rock; as a result, he's protected on three sides. Do you see? Only one of the Hydra's nine heads can get at him in that narrow space. Heracles has chosen the best possible place to fight."

"Oh, yes," Iolaus assured them, "my master is the greatest warrior in the history of the world. He has to be, or Hera would have succeeded in destroying him long ago."

As Heracles parried with the monster, Heracles seemed to fence with one of the Hydra's heads. The boy told them that the goddess Hera had even tried to kill Heracles when he was a baby. She had sent two poisonous snakes into his nursery. The baby Heracles had strangled both of them!

"But why does the goddess hate him?" asked Bridget.

"He is the illegitimate son of Zeus, and Hera is the wife of Zeus. She has tried many times to harm my master. So great is her hatred for him that, when we came to these swamps, the goddess sent a Giant Crab to kill Heracles. My master smashed it with his club."

"That explains why this swamp smells like crabmeat!" said Bridget.

"Look!" yelled Barnaby. One of the Hydra's heads darted forward; Heracles leaped back. The head was momentarily wedged in the cleft of the rock. The strong man brought his club down upon the head with so much force he smashed it to jelly.

The neck with the destroyed head retreated, but at once one of the other heads leapt forward to attack Heracles.

Admiringly, Barnaby said, "Do you see his strategy? Heracles is going to smash the heads one at a time until he destroys all nine of them!"

"But Barnaby," said Babette, "look there. Look at the stump that was once a head."

"Oh, no," said Bridget.

A strange thing happened, something that seemed impossible. The stump swelled and bulged. They watched in disbelief. The stump forked, then grew in two directions. From the stump emerged two new heads!

Heracles leaped forward, catching the snakelike head that was attacking him against the rocky face of the ledge with his foot. He swung his club with such ferocity that the sound of the blow echoed through the swamp.

"I know of certain reptiles and amphibians able to regenerate severed limbs," said Barnaby, "but I've never seen the process occur so quickly."

As Heracles parried with another head, the second stump swelled, forked, and produced two more heads.

"The monster now has eleven heads," said Iolaus sadly. "My master has destroyed two of them but the monster has not only replaced them but gained a pair."

"Heracles is losing ground," said Bridget. "We've got to do something. Beauregard, what can we do?"

Barnaby turned the pages of his guidebook. "There must be something useful in here."

"If nothing is done," said Iolaus, "eventually my master will grow exhausted. He will destroy many heads, but each time he smashes one of them, two more will grow. In the end, Heracles will tire. He is the strongest man on earth, the greatest of all warriors, but he is mortal. His strength will not last forever. Finally, his mighty arms will lose their strength; the Hydra will kill him. The goddess will win." The boy's chin trembled, but he did not weep. He began to descend the tree.

"He is my uncle," said Iolaus.

"Heracles is your uncle?"

"I must help him. If the Hydra kills him, it will have to kill me too."

"Wait!" Barnaby waved the little guidebook. "I've found something. Come on!" Barnaby started down the tree. "We've got to collect firewood. Hurry!"

The kids and Iolaus waded through the swamp, finding wood dry enough to build a fire.

"The way to keep the heads from regenerating," explained Barnaby, "is to cauterize the stumps with fire."

"Cauterize?" said Bridget. "What the heck does that mean?"

The fire blazed up. "You'll see," said Barnaby. "Here, Iolaus." Barnaby handed a burning branch to the boy. "You are the one who must help Heracles, not us."

Holding the blazing branch above his head, Iolaus ran to the tall spire of rock. So intent was the Hydra upon Heracles, it did not notice the boy behind it.

"He is very brave," said Babette admiringly.

Iolaus mounted the spire until he was very near to the Hydra. When Heracles succeeded in smashing another of the monster's heads, Iolaus leapt forward with the branch and applied its burning end to the stump.

"Hooray!" yelled Barnaby.

The stump steamed. The neck containing it reared backward.

"Does it work?" whispered Bridget.

No new pair of heads emerged. The trick worked! The kids cheered.

Each time Heracles smashed a head, Iolaus leapt forward with the burning branch. One head was destroyed, then another and another. Finally, only one was left.

"Something strange about that last head," said Barnaby. He leafed through his guidebook. "I was afraid of this," he said. "I remember now; the center head is different from the others. It is immortal."

"Immortal?" said Bridget.

"It cannot be killed."

"There must be some way!" said Babette.

Although Heracles was sometimes able to strike the last head with his club, his mighty blows did not destroy it. Each time it was struck, the head shuddered and withdrew. The blow caused it to suffer a terrible wound but, in a moment, the head healed itself and again attacked Heracles.

Barnaby ran forward. He waded through the swamp to the spire of rock. When he reached the spire, he yelled up to Iolaus.

"What is it?" Babette said. "What is Barnaby saying?"

The boy Iolaus climbed closer to where Heracles was standing. Barnaby began to make his way back through the swamp to the high place where the others were waiting.

"Look," Babette said, "Iolaus is shouting advice to Heracles!"

Heracles withdrew into the cleft of the rock. The monster battered the spire with its only remaining head. The necks containing the remains of the other heads writhed in the air like the arms of an octopus.

When Heracles emerged, he had put aside his club. Now, he carried the sword that had hung at his waist. The Hydra surged toward him, trying to catch the man between its jaws. Heracles leapt to one side, but the head struck a blow that flung him back into the cleft. The Hydra reared back to come at Heracles again, but Heracles scrambled to safety before it could crush him between its jaws. Heracles swung the sword with such speed it flashed in the sunlight. The Hydra tried again to kill him but this time Heracles leapt atop the head and straddled its neck. For a moment, he seemed to ride the Hydra as if it were a horse, but then Heracles twisted his body and raised his sword. He swung the sword with all his might and severed the neck.

The Hydra's head dropped. It bounced down the steep side of the spire of rock. Heracles ran down the spire after the head. It fell with a splash into the shallow water of the swamp. Heracles hefted an enormous boulder into the air and heaved it atop the head. The boulder shuddered. It moved on its foundation as if somehow the head beneath it was trying to push away the huge weight.

The Hydra's serpentlike body with its aura of necks slid down the spire of rock. The monster seemed to search blindly, stupidly for its head, then staggered and fell full-length into the mud of the swamp, sending up a splash of water. The monster's huge bulk trembled, writhed, then became still.

"Is—is it dead?" whispered Bridget.

"Hooray!" yelled Barnaby. He had told Iolaus how Heracles could defeat the final head, the immortal one, and Iolaus had carried the news to Heracles. Still, it seemed unbelievable that Heracles had finally defeated the monstrous Hydra.

Not far from where the mammoth creature lay in the mud, Heracles stood in the shallow water. To thank the gods for his victory, he raised his arms to the sky. The boy Iolaus ran to him, and they embraced. Iolaus broke away from Heracles, pointing to where Barnaby, Babette, Bridget, and Beauregard waited for them on a piece of high ground.

The hero and his nephew made their way toward them.

As Heracles approached, he struck Babette as surprisingly graceful in his movements. Bridget found him handsome and unbelievably muscular. All of them noticed his flashing teeth, his wide-open grin. They felt as if they were meeting a famous movie star and a handsome athlete all rolled into one person.

Heracles stopped in front of them and thanked them. Iolaus had told him of their help. "Is there any way I may return the favor? I see you are strangers, travellers from a land far away. No doubt you are on a quest? May I be of any assistance?"

Bridget spoke up, "Yes, as a matter of fact. Do you know where a girl named Persephone lives? We're looking for her."

"Persephone is the daughter of the goddess Demeter," said Babette. "We hope to save her."

"Yeah," said Barnaby, "we've come all this way to save her from Hades."

"Ah," Heracles wrinkled his brow, "very difficult. The goddess Demeter is said to live on an island. Perhaps you will find the girl there as well. Unfortunately, I do not know the whereabouts of Demeter's island."

"Oh, what a pity," said Babette.

"Besides," said Iolaus, "my master must be about his business. He must complete more Labors!"

"We mustn't be impolite, Iolaus," said Heracles. "These people have helped us. We must return the favor if at all possible. Let me ponder the problem." Heracles thought for awhile. "Do you know why the girl is in danger? Is Hades angry at her for some reason?"

"Oh, no," said Babette, "it is said the god Hades loves her. He is going to kidnap her. It is from that fate we want to save her."

"Ah, love. Well, then," the handsome hero smiled. "You see, this is very odd news. Hades is a cold and gloomy god, one who dwells in the underworld. Never has he shown the slightest interest in any girl, no matter how beautiful. I suspect, if Hades is in love, then that rascal Eros is responsible."

"AIR-oz?" Bridget repeated. "Who's he?"

Heracles smiled again. "A girl who has never heard of Eros and his magical arrows! You must come from a country that is very far away indeed!"

Babette told Bridget, "Eros is the boy-god, the one you Americans usually call Cupid."

"Oh," said Bridget, blushing. She felt a little dumb. Of course she had heard of Cupid.

Heracles said, "Eros is the son of Aphrodite." He said the name softly, reverentially: "Af-roh-DY-tee."

"I've heard of her," Bridget said. "The goddess of Love and Beauty."

"What I suggest is that you go to the Temple of Aphrodite. It may be that the goddess will help you. Implore her to intercede with Eros. If the boy-god can be prevented from sending one of his darts into Hades, then you can save this girl."

Barnaby asked, "But where will we find Aphrodite's temple?"

Heracles laughed. "Wonderful! Now, I can help you. It is not far from here. Iolaus," he turned to the boy, "you must lead them there."

"Yes, my master," said the boy.

"I must attend to my next Labor," said Heracles, "or I would guide you myself. But it is not far, a day's journey. Iolaus will lead you. But please, take my advice. Aphrodite is a true goddess. Take care never to offend her in any way."

"Don't worry about that!" said Barnaby.

"Good luck!" called Heracles.

"Well," said Iolaus, "if we want to be out of these swamps before sunset, we better get going!"

Chapter 4
The Dark Cave

So far as Bridget was concerned, Iolaus was acting a little weird. After adjusting her Yankees baseball cap so the bill faced backward, she gave Iolaus a long hard look. "See that?" she told Beauregard. "There he goes again." Iolaus was sitting beside the path, pulling a pebble out of his sandal. Then he coughed loudly. Too loudly. It all looked pretty fishy to Bridget. Was the boy ill? Did he really have a cold? Bridget doubted it.

Iolaus had been perfectly fine when they left Heracles. He had led Bridget, Beauregard, Barnaby, and Babette out of the Swamps of Lerna. No problem. He'd led them for a long walk, then found a place where they could spend the night. Iolaus had been a first-rate guide right up until an hour ago when he complained of a stomach ache. Then he developed an ear ache. Then he bruised his heel somehow. Then he saw a hawk swerve overhead and claimed it was a bad omen.

"You know what's wrong with him?" said Bridget to Beauregard. "I'll tell you my theory. He doesn't want to lead us there. He's scared."

"Couldn't you go on ahead to the Temple of Aphrodite without me?" said Iolaus. He was sitting beside the road with his head in his hands. "I feel terrible about delaying you."

"He's afraid all right," said Bridget. "What did I tell you?" She glowered at the boy. "Well, I've had enough." Bridget strode up to Iolaus and stood over him until he sighed and looked up at her. "What's wrong with you? And don't tell me your ears are ringing or your big toe hurts or anything else that's stupid. What are you afraid of?"

"Be nice to him, Bridget," Babette said. "He is only a boy."

"The Temple of Aphrodite is just down the road," Iolaus said. He bit his lower lip.

"Look me in the eye," Bridget said. "Have you been down this road?"

"No, not exactly."

"Then you don't even know if the Temple of Aphrodite is down there!"

"I think it is. Please, just let me stay here. I don't feel well, not at all!"

Babette gave Bridget a stern look and motioned her to go away. Bridget had many good qualities, but subtlety was not one of them. Bridget moved aside. Babette sat down beside Iolaus.

"Have you been down this road before, Iolaus?" she asked.

"I've been this far but no farther."

"With Heracles?"

"Yes."

"Did Heracles go farther down the road?"

"Yes!" The boy looked relieved. "You see, that's how I know the Temple of Aphrodite is down there. My master went to see Aphrodite. I waited right here until he came back. Please, couldn't I just wait here until you return?"

Babette called to the others. "Iolaus says it's just down the road." She put her arm around the boy. "If you don't feel well, you don't have to go with us. We'll be fine."

Bridget sniffed loudly.

"I've heard stories, that's all," said Iolaus. His ears were bright red. "About goddesses and, and—what they do."

"What sort of stories?"

Iolaus stood up. He seemed to have made a decision. "If you want to come face to face with a goddess, that's your business, but this is as far as I go. I apologize!" He started running down the road the way they had come, then suddenly stopped and turned around. "Just be careful!"

"I don't get it, Iolaus," said Barnaby. "I can't believe you are afraid. What could be down there that is more frightening than a nine-headed monster?" It was hard to believe that Iolaus was the same boy who had bravely helped Heracles fight the Hydra.

"Have you ever heard of Actaeon?" yelled the boy. As he pronounced each syllable, his voice seemed to go up an octave: "AK-tee-uhn," he said again, even more panicked. With that, he spun on his heel and ran off.

"Actaeon?" said Bridget. "Who the heck is Actaeon?"

"Mm," said Beauregard, "*Metamorphoses.*"

"Meta-what?" said Bridget.

Barnaby looked up Actaeon in the guidebook.

"*Metamorphoses* is a book," said Beauregard, "a most interesting one by the poet Ovid. The book is a collection of stories of humans who transform into one thing or another, usually because of a god. I am afraid the gods do have a dreadful tendency to turn mortals into brooks, birds, trees, all sorts of things. I believe you will find the sad story of Actaeon in Ovid's Metamorphoses."

"Actaeon!" yelled Barnaby. "I found it!" He quickly skimmed the page.

"Well," demanded Bridget, "who is he?"

"He was turned into a deer!" reported Barnaby.

"By the goddess Artemis, I believe," said Beauregard.

"Who?" asked Bridget. She wondered if she would ever be able to keep all these god and goddess names straight.

"AHR-tuh-mis," Babette said. "The Virgin Hunter."

To mark his place, Barnaby put his finger in the guidebook. "It says Actaeon was a young man. One day, he was out hunting with his dogs and his best friend, and he accidentally came upon the goddess Artemis. She was bathing in a pool. And he saw her."

Bridget laughed. "Saw her naked?"

"The offended goddess threw a handful of water at Actaeon, and he turned into a deer. That's what it says. No more did the drops of water hit him than hair sprouted all over his body. His nose grew long. Antlers sprouted from his forehead. His fingers and toes globbed together and turned into hooves."

"Wow. Just for accidentally looking at a goddess?"

"That's not the worst of it," said Beauregard. "Tell her the rest of the story, Barnaby."

Barnaby opened the book again and read what was written on the next page. "Oh, no! This is just awful!"

"What?" demanded Bridget. "What could be worse than being turned into a deer?"

Barnaby looked at her. "His own dogs found him."

"Now that," sniffed Beauregard, as his tail twitched almost involuntarily, "sounds like the beginning of a most unpleasant fate."

Barnaby nodded grimly. "Thinking Actaeon was a real deer, the dogs chased him, pulled him down. He couldn't speak to them, you see. His own dogs. And the worst of it was he was shot and killed by an arrow fired by his best friend!"

"I'll bet is was those dogs that revealed his presence to Artemis to begin with," said Beauregard. "Poor fellow. Then they turn on him. Typical canine blundering."

"Wow." Bridget looked up the road. "No wonder Iolaus got scared. All that just for accidentally looking at a goddess."

She wished she had some bubble gum. She'd used up her last piece last night. "Goddesses must be really touchy."

All of them frowned. They were not accustomed to feeling afraid, but the story of the fate of Actaeon did make them uneasy.

"Keep in mind," said Bridget at last, "that's a story about the goddess Artemis, not the goddess Aphrodite."

"That's right," said Barnaby. "Aphrodite is supposed to be the goddess of love and beauty, isn't she? She must be much nicer than the goddess Artemis."

"Well, she certainly is more beautiful," said Babette thoughtfully.

The others looked at one another.

"Come on!" yelled Bridget. "Are we going to save Persephone and end winter, or not?"

"Hey, do you guys hear something?" asked Barnaby.

The others listened.

Clang! Clang! Clang!

What was it? Not far ahead of them, someone was pounding on metal.

Led by Babette and Beauregard, the group moved toward the noise. They climbed a hill, then descended the other side.

"Look!" whispered Barnaby. "It's a cave."

Clouds of smoke drifted from the mouth of the cave. As they came closer, the hammering grew louder until it was nearly deafening. They also heard intermittent whooshing sounds, as if inside the cave lived an asthmatic whale.

"Hold it right there!" cried a high-pitched voice.

The hammering ceased.

"Who is it, Head?" called a deep baritone voice. "Is someone out there?"

The whale, or whatever it was, continued to wheeze.

An expert at karate, Babette assumed a combat-ready pose and entered the cave first.

"Can you see anything?" Barnaby asked.

Bridget entered the cave after Babette. Beauregard and Barnaby followed.

Babette whispered, "In ancient Greece, travelers are supposed to be well-treated."

"I sure hope so," whispered Bridget.

"It was considered a sin or a crime to mistreat a visitor," said Babette. "I am sure of it."

"I can't see a thing," said Barnaby.

"Hey!" yelled Bridget. "Anybody home?"

"Could we beg a cup of water?" called Babette in her most polite voice. They were now inside the cave. "We've traveled a long distance and are terribly thirsty."

"No kidding," said Bridget. "My mouth feels like the beach at Coney Island."

The cavernous space of the cave was filled with the glowing light produced by a forge.

Two slender, golden figures were operating a bellows. The bellows was producing the whooshing sound. The smoke from the fire was so thick that it was difficult to make out what all the cave contained. Pieces of iron, bronze weapons, wooden wheels, contraptions of one sort or another were piled up everywhere.

"Take care of them, Table!" yelled the deep voice. The hammering resumed.

From one of the dark recesses of the cave, a three-legged table atop golden wheels rolled toward Barnaby and the others. No one pushed it. The wheeled table rolled by itself!

Atop the table was a small jug filled to the brim with water.

"That thing moves by itself!" said Bridget. "It must be some kind of robot."

To see better, Babette lifted her sunglasses.

Barnaby continued to stare at the tripod table in amazement. "How can it possibly operate? By batteries?" The table glided closer to them.

In the further recesses of the cave, beyond the first forge, they saw more forges attended by more of the elegant golden women. "They're robots!" exclaimed Bridget. "Like that guy in Star Wars—C3-P0!"

The self-propelled table carrying the jug of water glided to a stop in front of Bridget. "You think I should drink it?" she asked the others. "Maybe it's poison."

"Go on, my dear," said Beauregard. "I can tell by the smell it is fresh, pure water."

Bridget picked up the jug and took a sip. "Wow, it's delicious!" She drank deeply until her thirst was quenched, then set down the jug with a thump. "Hey!"

The others looked at her. Bridget was staring at the jug as if it were haunted.

"I must have drunk a third of the water in the jug," Bridget explained. "No kidding. But look!" She pointed at the jug. "It's brim full!"

In fact, the jug was full. It was hard to believe Bridget had drunk any of it. "It must be magical," said Babette, "it refills whenever anyone drinks from it. If you study mythology, you will discover many stories about similar jugs. The gods often give them to people they like."

"Hello?" Beauregard called. "We thank you kindly for the water."

"Can you see anyone else back there?" Barnaby peered into the back of the cave. The dimly lit cavern seemed to go on and on forever. They could barely see a bent-over figure, a large man hammering upon something.

"Who is it?" whispered Bridget. They took a few steps farther into the cave.

"Can it be Hephaestus?" whispered Babette. "I wonder if this could be his workshop."

"Far enough!" cried the high-pitched voice. "Take another step at your peril!"

All of them froze.

Not far from where they stood, setting on top of another three-legged table was a head. It was a golden head that might have been male or female. It was hard to tell. The head was unconnected to any body. It set atop the table as if it were a vase.

The hammering ceased.

"Of course, he is Hephaestus. Who are you?" demanded the head. "How dare you come here? And do not bother to lie. I can spot a liar. This is the smithy of Hephaestus the god, my master. Anyone who trespasses here without per-mission, anyone who dares to steal any of my master's goods, will live to regret it." The golden lips of the head snapped together, reminding the kids of a purse clicking shut.

"We are travelers from a faraway land," called Babette. "We are here on a quest. And we certainly won't trespass," she took a step backward. "Or steal." She put her hands behind her back. "But we do have a question to ask Hephaestus. We need to ask him for directions."

"Is that so?" The head seemed about to make a speech but stopped before it could do much more than open and close its mouth.

"Travelers?" said the deep voice. "Quest?" From out of the back of the cave hobbled a very dirty and ugly blacksmith. On his legs, he wore golden braces. To support himself, he leaned upon a golden crutch.

Babette knelt. The others did too, even Bridget.

The god Hephaestus really was kind of ugly. He had thick black hair, made greasy by the work that he did. His bearded face was smeared with soot and grease. His upper body was immensely strong. His shoulders, neck and chest were as muscular as those of Heracles. But his legs were spindly. If not supported by the golden braces, they seemed likely to collapse under the weight of Hephaestus. A god who was ugly? A god who was lame? It seemed impossible. Yet, all of them felt instinctively that they were in the presence of a being immensely powerful and important.

The god Hephaestus stopped in front of Barnaby, reached down and plucked off Barnaby's glasses. He inspected them curiously.

"They are corrective eyeglasses, sir," said Barnaby. "Those metals are alloys, and the lenses are made of plastic."

"Hmm," murmured the god.

"You know, I am tremendously interested in your work," continued Barnaby. "Of all the gods and goddesses, you are the one I most admire. I wonder if we could look around?"

The god returned his glasses.

"That horse, for example." Barnaby put his glasses back on. "It is a horse, isn't it? A mechanical horse."

In one of the cave's recesses was a life-sized mechanical horse missing one golden leg. It was upon this leg that Hephaestus had been hammering when the kids had approached his smithy.

"It's Pegasus," murmured Babette. "A mechanical Pegasus!" Indeed, the golden horse did seem to be a duplicate of Pegasus, the famous winged horse.

Pleased by their interest in his work, the god let them inspect the horse. It was dreamily beautiful. The gold that covered it seemed soft and warm as real flesh. The mechanical horse was so realistic, so detailed, that despite its golden color, it seemed alive. They expected it to look at them, to snort and whinny.

Hephaestus led them farther into his smithy. He showed them a mechanical chair that looked to be some sort of trap. When someone sat down on it, bars sprang out and encased the sitter.

"But what was it used for?" asked Barnaby. "If you don't mind my asking, I mean." He did not want to offend the god. He vividly remembered the story of the young man who was turned into a deer. Hephaestus merely smiled. "I once desired to know something," he murmured, but would say no more.

Babette looked thoughtful but said nothing.

Hephaestus showed them a bronze hunting net. Although made of metal, its strands were fine as gossamer threads. They glowed faintly in the light of the forges.

"It is like a glow-in-the-dark spider web!" said Bridget.

"Look here," said the god. "Of course, it is only a model." He showed them a woman made of clay. "Her name is Pandora."

"Pandora!" exclaimed Barnaby. "She's beautiful!"

"She was the most beautiful mortal woman on earth," said Babette. "Do you know the story?"

All of them remembered it. The god Hephaestus had made Pandora of clay. Commanded to do so by Zeus, he had made this model, then a second one even more beautiful. The Four Winds had breathed life into it. But Pandora was as foolish as she was beautiful. She was given a chest and told never to open it. Of course, Pandora opened it the first chance she got. Out flew all the Spites that harm and torment human beings: Old Age, Sickness, Madness, Anger, Headache. From that day forward, human beings had to suffer. But at the bottom of the chest lay one good and beautiful thing: Hope.

It hardly seemed possible that there had ever really been a Pandora, yet here was a version of her, a clay model so beautiful that it was hard to look at her and not fall into a swoon.

The god showed them many other wondrous objects, too many to describe. He showed them so many dazzling creations that they worked up quite a thirst and had to call again for the magical jug of water.

"And why have you come so far?" Hephaestus asked them when they had finished drinking. "Whom do you seek?"

"We come from another time, another land," said Babette.

The god nodded wisely as if he had no trouble understanding how this could be true.

"We are on a quest," Babette continued.

"Yeah," said Barnaby, "we're trying to save an innocent girl named Persephone. She's in plenty of danger!"

"Please, don't interrupt me, Barnaby," Babette said. Barnaby did have a terrible tendency to interrupt. She explained to Hephaestus what Heracles had told them, that if Hades was about to fall in love with Persephone, then Eros must be responsible. "We hope Aphrodite will tell Eros to leave Hades alone. We think if she will help us, we can prevent this disaster from occurring. So if you will be so kind as to tell us where the Temple of Aphrodite is, we will be on our way." She smiled winningly.

"Head!" called the god.

The tripod table containing the golden head rolled forward.

"Yes, my master?" said the head.

"You will go with these young mortals."

"With these mortals, but, but—"The head clanked its lips unhappily.

"Show them the way to my wife's temple." The god nodded to Babette. "I would show you the way myself except that

I must finish my mechanical horse. Soon, it will be ready to fly." He looked back at the golden horse as if eager to return to his work.

"But, my lord," said the head, "they are mortals. You don't mean it!"

Hephaestus found a basket, deposited the head unceremoniously into it, and handed the basket to Barnaby. "Head will help you. There's little need to bring her back. I have plenty more." The god gestured at his golden women. The kids realized the head must be an unfinished robot-servant of some sort. "Take care of them, Head. It is my wish that they do not come to harm."

"Grrr!" murmured the head. It did not seem at all pleased to be given away. "Come on then!" said the head. "Let's be on our way!"

"Thank you, sir!" said Barnaby.

"Thanks a million!" said Bridget.

"*Merci beaucoup!*" said Babette.

Beauregard bowed graciously.

"We haven't all day!" said the head. "Come on!"

Chapter 5
The Goddess of Love

Barnaby, Bridget, Babette, and Beauregard soon discovered why Hephaestus was so willing to give up the golden head. It chattered constantly. In fact, it would not shut up. The head gossiped; it whined and complained. It predicted dark disaster. Mainly, it rattled on and on about the goddess Aphrodite. The head did not approve of Aphrodite. Certainly not. "The goddess is not good enough for Hephaestus. She is not good enough for any truly decent god, but especially Hephaestus. He is my creator, you know." The head rolled its eyes and made its golden lips snap together as if to say, "What more need be said? I ask you."

So far as Head was concerned, the list of Aphrodite's crimes was endless. "His wife! If she can be called one! Aphrodite has by my count seven children. Three are by Ares, one by Hermes, two by Poseidon, and one by Dionysius." The head viciously snapped her lips three times as if biting pieces out of the air. "None of her children is by my master. None! Can you believe it? Oh, Aphrodite's wickedness! Her infidelities! The stories I could tell you. The scandals! And yet, Hephaestus forgives her. So kind, so warm is my master's heart. But everyone forgives her. Everyone! It isn't fair. Not a bit. Especially men. They take one look at her and lose whatever common sense they had to begin with. Aphrodite's beautiful, isn't she? So she is to be forgiven anything! Men are weak. And women are not much better. They can't help themselves. Everyone worships Aphrodite. Everyone! Well, I don't, of course! You'll see. But I am not mortal. Thank goodness."

Head rolled her eyes to the left, producing a loud click; then she rolled them to the right and produced another click. "And that wild-boy son of hers, Eros!" It turned out that once, in a playful mood, Eros had tossed Head up into a tree, where she had remained for several years. A heavy rain had caused Head's jaw to rest shut, so she had been unable to call out for help. "I'd be there still but fortunately one afternoon my master saw me glint in the sunlight."

The kids did not say anything, but all of them thought the same thing: If Head's jaws would once again rust shut, it would not be an altogether bad thing.

The theme of Aphrodite's misdeeds was the head's favorite topic, but she also loved to talk about Hephaestus, about the god's brilliance, about the splendid palaces he constructed, the indestructible sword blades he forged, and his numerous magical inventions.

"Why is Olympus so spectacular? Because of my master. Who do you suppose made all those palaces, the homes of the gods and goddesses? Do you suppose anyone else could have built so many splendors, even Apollo? Don't be absurd. Only my master is capable of creating such works—detailed, radiant, unforgettable. And why?" The head lowered her voice. "Because of what Zeus did to him."

"What happened?" asked Bridget. Ever since she had first met him, Bridget had wondered why, alone among the gods, Hephaestus was ugly and lame, but of course it would have been rude to ask.

"From the beginning, he's been mistreated. The most worthy of all the gods! My master was born weak, homely, so what did his mother do?"

"Who was Hephaestus's mother?" asked Bridget.

"Hera! She took one look at him, the poor weak little thing, and tossed him out of Olympus as if he were a piece of trash! Can you imagine? His own mother! Fortunately, he fell into the ocean and was unharmed."

"But about his crippled legs—?"

"Of course, once Hera discovered that Hephaestus made beautiful jewelry, the goddess became interested in him and set him up in a smithy. Twenty bellows, working day and night. That is why he invented the mechanical women, to assist him. You cannot believe the amount of jewelry Hera requires. And Aphrodite!" Head rolled her eyes, producing the clicks. "That is how they exploit him. You have no idea how hard he works. Like a slave. Not that Aphrodite appreciates him. He works day and night, but she has never worked a moment of her life! He adores her, but do you think she cares?"

"But his legs?" insisted Bridget. "Those golden braces?"

"Oh, cruel, cruel Zeus! One day, when Zeus punished Hera, Hephaestus jumped up to defend his mother. There you see his bravery. Zeus flung him from Olympus. My poor master fell for nine days and nine nights! Onto stone! And that is why to this day my master is crippled and—and—" the head's golden lips trembled, "and somewhat less than attractive. But, you see, that is why he is the most creative of all the gods. Do you understand? Because they hurt him, because they exploit him, my master cannot bear this cruel, cruel world. With his skill, he manufactures a new and better world. For this reason, all artists love him—goldsmiths, sculptors, painters, architects. All mortals who create beauty worship the lame Hephaestus. Do you see? Do you understand? Oh, dear!" The head fell back into the basket. "There is the temple. Hide me! Don't let her see me!"

As they approached the temple, the group noticed an amazing change that seemed to come from the air itself. The fragrant air around the Temple of Aphrodite was not like ordinary air. There was something tender about it. Nor was the light around the temple ordinary. It was the light that makes the world radiant near the end of the day, just after the sun drops behind the horizon. In the fragrant air, in the tender light, Bridget, Barnaby, and Babette became happier, healthier, and more good-looking. When they glanced at Barnaby, Bridget and Babette were astonished to see that he was handsome. When he looked at Babette and Bridget, the young man was astounded to see how beautiful they were. He had never really noticed before. Beauregard's black fur grew thicker and glossier than ever.

When the kids saw the Temple of Aphrodite, they stopped in their tracks. The most beautiful building they had ever seen was made of gold and ivory, silver and alabaster. It seemed to float. Faint, lovely music came from somewhere within it. The temple's walls were covered with pictures of loving couples. The painted lovers held hands; they kissed; they walked along beaches.

"It is a dream," said Babette.

"That temple can't be real," said Bridget.

"Look," whispered Barnaby, "is it my imagination, or are those doors opening?"

The doors were tall and white and elegant. Each one was carved with an image of Aphrodite rising from the sea, standing gracefully atop a giant scallop shell. The kids recognized the image of the goddess standing in the shell, but where had they seen it before? "Ah," said Beauregard, "it is the famous image of the goddess painted by the Italian Botticelli. Venus on the Half Shell, it is called, in jest of course."

Suddenly, it became clear that, in fact, one of the doors was opening; it opened very slowly and only part of the way. Was it the goddess? Bridget, Babette, Barnaby, and Beauregard froze. They remembered the terrible fate of the young man who had come upon a goddess unaware; they recalled how Iolaus had fled rather than accompany them to Aphrodite's temple.

Beauregard made a slight yelp of surprise. Something emerged from between the doors. "My goodness, it can't be," whispered Beauregard.

"A cat!" said Bridget. "In a toga!"

In fact, the cat looked amazingly like Beauregard. He was tall and glossy black. If he had not been wearing the toga, he could have passed for Beauregard's identical twin.

Beauregard ran forward. The other cat stood still; both of them rose up on their hind legs. The two cats stared at each other, nose to nose.

"Are they going to fight?" asked Babette. Just in case it was necessary, she assumed a fighting pose. But the two cats embraced warmly.

"Beauregard!" said the strange cat. "I thought you'd turn up eventually. Lovely to see you!"

"Branwell?" whispered Bridget. "It's Beauregard's cousin Branwell! But how'd he get here?"

"I didn't even know Beauregard had a cousin," said Barnaby.

"Oh, no!" yelled Bridget. "We completely forgot!"

"Forgot what?" asked the bewildered Barnaby.

"Branwell was coming to visit on the same day we started this crazy adventure! We completely forgot about him!"

Beauregard brought his cousin over to see the others. Branwell did bear a remarkable resemblance to Beauregard. It turned out that Branwell had arrived at Bridget's apartment door shortly after Beauregard and the kids had taken off to visit Cue Ball's curio shop.

"I caught your scent, old boy," Branwell told Beauregard, "and tracked you to the East Village, some shop presided over by a bald man."

"Cue Ball!" said Bridget.

"I managed to sneak into a hidden room in the back and found a big cabinet."

"The Cabinet of Hephaestus," said Babette.

"I could tell by my nose you'd gone into it but couldn't figure out how to get it open. Finally I touched the carved image of—" Branwell motioned at the large image of Aphrodite rising from the sea carved on the temple door. "Well, it looked just like that one, except it was smaller. The cabinet doors swung open; I ran in. They slammed shut behind me, and a minute later, I found myself right here, where we are standing now."

"Who is it?" said Head, from inside the reed basket.

Branwell cocked an ear. "Pardon me, but I believe I just heard your basket say something."

"You did!" said Bridget. She whispered loudly, "It's just Head."

"Did you say," Branwell tilted his head to one side, "Head?"

"Go on. Show him, Babette."

Babette opened the basket and tilted it so that Head and Branwell could see one another.

"How disappointing," said Head. "Why, you are nothing but a mere cat."

"And you seem to be a mere head," said Branwell. "Oh, I beg your pardon. Have you lost the rest of you? Perhaps we can help you find it?" Like Beauregard, Branwell possessed excellent manners and would not have dreamed of hurting Head's feelings, even if the head had just insulted the feline race.

"I have never missed my body," said Head. "Lack of limbs is the reason I am entirely sensible."

"Really?" murmured Branwell. "Well, to each his own, I suppose."

Beauregard slapped his forehead with a paw. "Where are my manners? Let me introduce everyone." After he completed the introductions, Beauregard told his cousin, "We'd better fill you in on what we're doing here. Branwell, we're on a quest."

"That does sound fun."

"Yeah," said Bridget, "to end winter."

"How interesting," said Branwell. He stroked his whiskers. "Like most of my species, I have never cared for the season."

The kids explained their mission to save Persephone.

Branwell listened thoughtfully but jumped slightly when he heard the name Persephone. "But I've heard that name."

"That name? You mean, Persephone?"

"In fact, I've heard very little else since arriving here. Aphrodite is in a fury about her. Persephone, Persephone, Persephone! The goddess is in a perfect rage."

"A fury?" asked Babette. "A rage? That doesn't sound good, not at all. Are you sure?"

Come along. I'll show you. Now, you must be very quiet. Since I am a guest here, I'm allowed to come and go as I please, but there are limits. Aphrodite is a goddess, you know. And these holy ones are—well, as you know, it does not do to infuriate the powerful."

From the basket, Head declared, "If we are going to enter the temple, close up my basket."

"Why, Head," said Babette, looking down at her, "you sound terribly uneasy. Are you afraid of something?"

"Of course I am. You would be too if you had any sense. If you must know, I am in danger each time I come near her."

"Her?"

"Aphrodite. Why do you suppose I no longer have a body?"

"We did kind of wonder." The kids exchanged glances.

"Aphrodite despises all of us mechanical women. Oh, you can't believe how jealous she can be. The last time I was sent here—I had to make a delivery for my master—I had a body like anyone else. She made it disappear! Out of mere spite!"

"My goodness."

"I had to roll home! The most undignified event of my life."

The kids tried not to laugh.

"And not long after that, Eros flung me into a tree. So please, when you meet the goddess, keep my basket closed. On no account let her know I am inside it. There's no telling what she might do if she discovers I am here."

After Babette closed the basket, Branwell led them through the temple doors into the most elegant arrangement of small, intimate rooms they had ever seen. Each room was lined with satin and contained a comfortable couch. Small tables held golden vases full of fragrant flowers. "As you can see," said Branwell, "the goddess of Love surrounds herself with beauty."

Babette whispered, "Hephaestus and Aphrodite are such an odd couple. He is ugly, and Aphrodite is beautiful. They are truly a union of opposites. His smithy is dark and smoky, but Aphrodite's temple is fragrant and full of light. Hephaestus is the god of hard work, but his wife is associated only with play and pleasure."

From the basket came a loud snap as if Head had tried to bite something.

"Sshh," said Branwell, "this way."

In the center of the temple was an open-air courtyard lined with slender columns. Graceful plants grew up out of stone pots. Attractive benches, just big enough for two, were tucked between the columns. But the most striking feature of the courtyard was a long rectangular pool of pure and sparkling water, just as blue as the sky it reflected. At its far end, they saw two figures.

"Aphrodite and Eros," Babette murmured.

Later, Head informed them that the goddess had not been wearing her girdle. That was the only reason the kids had not completely lost their senses. The girdle was not one of those peculiar undergarments worn by the overweight; it was a magical sash. When she wore her magical girdle, the beautiful goddess became totally irresistible. Not even Zeus could resist Aphrodite's charms at such times. Fortunately, when they saw her talking angrily to Eros, the goddess had not been wearing the girdle. It was possible to gaze at her and think rationally. Even without the magic girdle, Aphrodite's beauty was so overwhelming that the kids became speechless at sight of her. Barnaby turned bright red; his mouth fell open. Babette and Bridget looked at Aphrodite and thought of supermodels, of Cindy Crawford, Naomi Campbell, of Marilyn Monroe and Michelle Pfieffer. The goddess was superhumanly, impossibly beautiful. Also, she was angry.

The boy-god Eros did not seem to care greatly what mood his mother was in. A beautiful lad with a mischievous expression, he lay on the tiles beside the pool, dangled his fingers in the glittering water, and paid no particular attention to his mother.

The kids were so astonished to see the goddess that they could hardly concentrate on what she was saying. Something about Persephone and Demeter. What was it? They hid behind an enormous stone vase and listened intently.

"What? Demeter's daughter, engaged to Apollo! It cannot be! I will not allow it. Was I consulted? Does Zeus dare to insult me? I am the goddess of Love, am I not? I was not consulted. Besides, this little nobody, Persephone, she is no one special and hardly deserves to be wed to Apollo. If anyone should have handsome Apollo, it is—well, never mind. If only I had not been wed to that ugly dullard, Hephaestus. In any case, Demeter will not get away with it." The goddess nudged Eros with her toe. "Eros, pay attention! I have thought of a plan. You are to find Hades, shoot an arrow into him—make him love this snip of a girl, Persephone."

"Hades, old Hades in love!" Intrigued and amused, the boy-god sat up. "The god of the Dead, madly in love with Persephone!" Eros laughed at the thought. "What an idea!"

"Do it at once, fly, go! We haven't much time. Who knows how soon the wedding of Persephone and Apollo will be? And once they are married—well, it must not be! I will not allow it."

Eros hesitated. "Isn't it dangerous to offend so many gods? Demeter, Apollo, Zeus?"

"Are you a coward? Is any god greater than love? Even Hades? Is death greater than love? This is an excellent opportunity to demonstrate the supreme power of love. The other gods need to be taught that you and I are the most powerful of all the holy ones."

Eros nodded thoughtfully, "Well, when you put it that way . . ."

"I will take care of Demeter. Don't you worry. She won't dare interfere with my plans. And I will handle Zeus too, if the need arises. Do not worry."

"And Apollo?" asked Eros.

"Bah! What does the sun-god care? He will do as Zeus commands. I don't even believe he cares for the girl, not a bit. And why should he? He has all of Olympus at his feet! Now, go! Fly! Do you want the handsomest of all the gods to wed a nobody? A girl homely as a pig?"

Eros wrapped his arms around his knees. "You do go on, Mother. The girl is not homely. I have seen her. Persephone is almost as beautiful as you are—more beautiful, some might say."

"Bah! Silence!" The goddess's large eyes blazed with anger at this reference to Persephone's beauty. "Go! Fly! Find Hades and do as I say."

The boy-god rose to his feet. He spread his wings, then closed them. "I do not care to enter Hades' Kingdom. There, in the underworld, he is all-powerful. Not even Zeus likes to visit Hades in the underworld. When the father-god has a message for his brother Hades, he sends Hermes."

The goddess elevated her chin, displaying her graceful neck. "Even Hades occasionally tires of the company of the dead. Wait outside the gates of the underworld. When Hades emerges, you know what to do."

Eros smiled and pretended to be confused. "Should I deliver your compliments to the Dark King, Mother?"

"Fire an arrow into his hard heart!"

"Ha!" the boy-god laughed and leapt into the air. "Good-bye, my mother!"

"There," hissed Head from inside her basket, "you hear how malicious she is. What a trouble maker. I completely disapprove of love, as do all sensible people. Aphrodite and Eros have entirely too much power."

"Well," whispered Branwell, "hadn't we better be tiptoeing out of here?"

"Yeah," Bridget agreed, "it looks like it's not going to do any good to talk to her. Who knew she hated Persephone?"

"But how beautiful she is," murmured Barnaby. He gazed dreamily at the goddess.

"Come on, snap out of it!" Bridget gave Barnaby a nudge with her elbow. "Are you nuts? We gotta get out of here before she sees us!"

"He is under the spell of love," whispered Babette.

They all began to sneak away from the courtyard. Unfortunately, Barnaby could not resist looking back, hoping to catch one more glimpse of the beautiful Aphrodite. Not watching where he was going, he walked backward, tripped over his own big feet, and fell hard against a vase. It crashed to the tiles, spilling dirt and flowers, and breaking into twenty pieces.

"Barnaby!" yelped Bridget. "Now you've done it!" All of them froze, but it was too late. In a moment, the goddess stood before them.

"Ah, Branwell, I see you have brought guests here," the goddess smiled, "without my permission."

To be so close to the goddess was overwhelming. If she had seemed beautiful before, Aphrodite now seemed twice as beautiful. Her perfect skin was supple and radiant. Her hair seemed made of liquid fire. Her eyes—the kids hardly dared to look into her eyes.

The goddess called out a command to someone inside the temple. A beautiful girl appeared.

"Handmaiden, bring me my girdle," said the goddess. The girl scampered back into the temple.

"Oh, no!" From within the basket came a groan of despair. "Not the girdle!"

"Open that basket," ordered the goddess. "At once!"

When Babette hesitated, Aphrodite made a gesture. The basket lid opened by itself!

"Hello, Head," said Aphrodite. "So, it is you. Have you forgotten I have forbidden you ever again to come here?"

The golden head opened its eyes wide, then lowered them humbly. "I beg your pardon, holy one. I came at the command of my master, your husband."

The goddess ceased to smile.

"These are travelers from a distant land," Head explained. "Hearing of your great beauty, they have come all this way to worship at your feet. At Hephaestus' command, I merely guided them here to your temple."

"It is my fault, holy one," said Branwell quickly. "It was I who led them into the temple. I let them bring Head in the basket."

Barnaby attempted to speak, but Aphrodite's beauty had so overpowering an effect on him, all he could do was blush and stammer.

"Am I really so beautiful?" asked the goddess.

Barnaby nodded violently.

"Oh yes," said Beauregard. "Oh my, yes. Obviously you are the most beautiful goddess in the world—I mean, in the entire universe!"

Carrying a silken length of brightly colored cloth, the pretty handmaiden returned. She stood at Aphrodite's elbow.

The goddess took the cloth from the girl. She draped the magical girdle over her shoulder and around her slender waist. It shimmered and changed color like a rainbow.

"Perhaps I will forgive you for coming here, Head. Poor Head, always so sad. I have always thought it a pity, Head, that you have never experienced love." She took the basket from Babette, reached inside it and stroked Head's golden forehead, then bent down and kissed Head.

"Oh, no, please, holy one," Head gasped.

Aphrodite closed the basket lid and laughed. "Here, please take her." She gave the basket to Barnaby. "You must be very careful. When the basket is again opened, Head will fall in love with the first thing she sees." From inside the basket came a low moan. Aphrodite tilted back her beautiful head and laughed loudly.

One hour later, the kids blinked and shook their heads and pinched themselves. They felt as if they were waking from a long dream. Had they really met the goddess Aphrodite? Had they talked to her? Had they heard her musical voice? Was it possible that everywhere the goddess set her foot, a flower sprang up? Could she have been so beautiful? Her hair, those brilliant and mischievous eyes, that impossibly lovely mouth! They felt as if they had visited heaven, and now abruptly found themselves back on earth.

"Are you guys okay?" asked Bridget. "I'm not sure I am."

"Yes. Maybe. I think so," said Barnaby. He looked a little pale, as if he might be coming down with something.

"Psst," whispered a high-pitched voice. "Are we out of the temple?"

Barnaby looked down at the basket in his arms. He'd forgotten he was carrying it. They were standing on the road back to Hephaestus' cave. "Yes," he said. "I just can't remember how we got here. Does anybody?"

"Is that you, Head?" asked Beauregard.

"Is the goddess gone?"

"Yes, Aphrodite is gone," said Babette. "I feel a little dizzy." She removed her sunglasses and rubbed her eyes.

"Oh, I knew this would happen," Head said.

"What? What happened?" asked Barnaby. "I can't think. Here, Head, I'll open the basket."

"No, don't you dare!" Head yelled. "Don't open the basket!"

Barnaby hesitated. His fingers were on the basket's latch.

"What happened?" Head yelled. "I'll tell you what happened. All of you fell in love with Aphrodite the moment she put on the magic girdle. You know you did!"

"She is impossible to resist," murmured Babette. "So beautiful, so lovely. Those arms, those eyes!"

"She questioned you," Head cried. "And don't open the basket!"

"Don't open it?" Barnaby said. He let go of the latch. "I can't seem to remember why not."

"You told her everything. Everything! You told her you came here on a quest to save Persephone from Hades! And now, if that lid is opened, I will fall in love with the first person I see!"

"We did?" Barnaby said weakly. "You will?"

"She made you vow never to warn Demeter or Persephone, not by word or by deed."

"We did promise," groaned Bridget. "It's coming back to me now."

So irresistible had Aphrodite been once she had put on her magical girdle that all of them had lost their wits. They had fallen hopelessly in love with the goddess and told her everything she had asked. So great was the power of love that they forgot all their plans. All they wanted to do was please Aphrodite, to see her smile and laugh.

Now they stood in the harsh sunlight, half a mile from the temple. Everything had gone wrong. Worst of all, they had promised not to warn Persephone. They had taken a vow.

"What the heck are we going to do now?" moaned Bridget.

"Not only that," said Head, "but she's kept Branwell for a hostage. If you ever want to see that cat again, you'd better not cross her."

The kids were shocked. Was it possible?

"This is terrible!" exclaimed Babette.

"What are we going to do now?" wailed Bridget. She too felt terrible.

"Our only hope," said Beauregard, "is to get to Demeter's Island before Hades does. We must get there first and warn Persephone."

"But how?" asked Barnaby. "We don't even know where it is. And we've taken a vow. And Aphrodite's got Branwell."

"Listen carefully," said the golden head. "I have an idea. And whatever you do, don't open that basket!"

Chapter 6
The Storm

Head's idea, although a good one, was not quite as good as everyone had hoped.

"Carry me back to my master." Head was shut up inside the basket, but it was possible to hear her voice. The basket was sitting in the dirt beside the path that led to Hephaestus's cave.

"Okay," said Bridget.

"Once there, fling open the basket's lid and show me to my master. I will at once fall in love with Hephaestus."

Bridget looked at the basket. "Go on. You'll fall in love with him, then what?"

"That's it," said Head. "That is my idea in its entirety."

"But what good does that do us?" demanded Bridget. "We need to get to Demeter's Island."

From the basket came an angry snap. "My master ordered me to guide you to Aphrodite's temple. At great risk to myself, I did so. Now, I am through with you. Please, carry me back to my master."

Bridget frowned and balled up her fists as if she wanted to thump the basket containing Head.

"But look here, Head," said Babette, "as Bridget says, we need to get to Demeter's Island."

"That's right," said Barnaby. "We can't just give up."

"Do as you please," said Head. "But first, return me to my master. I have had more than enough adventure. If you ask me, next to love, the craving for adventure is the cause of most of the misery in the world."

"For pete's sake!" said Bridget.

All of them sat on the side of the dusty path. They felt depressed. How were they to get to Demeter's Island? Even if they did find a way there, they had no idea how they could help Persephone since they had promised Aphrodite not to warn the girl that Hades was coming to kidnap her. Besides, Aphrodite was holding Branwell as a hostage.

"We need a boat," said Barnaby.

"Even if we found a boat," said Babette, "who would steer it?"

"Even if we found someone to pilot it," said Bridget, "how would we know which way to go? We don't even have a map." She kicked a little at the basket.

"Even if we had a boat, someone to steer, and a map," said Beauregard, "it would take days to sail to Demeter's Island, wherever it is. And by then, Hades will have kidnapped Persephone." He wiggled his whiskers.

From inside the basket, Head said, "Obviously, your quest is hopeless. If you have any sense, you'll give up and go home. But first take me back to Hephaestus."

"We've never given up," said Barnaby. "No matter how much trouble we got into."

"We're not the sort of kids who give up!" said Bridget.

"Certainly not," said Beauregard. "The very idea!" He swished his long tail.

"If only we possessed a boat," said Babette.

They all sighed and looked down at their feet.

"Are vows really all that important?" Bridget gestured with her hands. "I mean, we didn't really sign anything. Maybe we could just go there and tell Persephone."

From inside the basket, Head snapped her lips in horror.

"In this world," said Babette, "vows are terribly important, especially vows made to a god. Don't you agree, Beauregard?"

Beauregard nodded. "I'm afraid so, Bridget. The gods are the enforcers of vows. They take a dim view of anyone who breaks them."

"But it was under duress!" Bridget kicked at the dirt with her tennis shoe. "Aphrodite practically forced us to take a vow. She wore that magic girdle. We didn't have a chance. If there's one thing I hate, it's unfairness!"

"I don't think that really qualifies as duress," said Babette. "We took a vow, and we have to stick to it." She folded her arms and gave Bridget a stern look.

Barnaby sighed. He looked down the road toward Hephaestus's cave and wished he had some idea where Demeter's Island was located. "Head," he said and looked down at the basket, "do you actually know the way to the island?"

From the basket came a noise as if Head might be grinding her teeth. "Even if I do, I don't see what difference it makes. I have not the slightest intention of going there. The very idea of a sea voyage makes me ill. Imagine if I were to fall overboard. I'd sink to the bottom and spend eternity sunk in mud, nosed by curious fish. No, thank you!"

Barnaby rubbed his chin. "There must be some way." Then he wiggled his fingers as he sometimes did when he got an exciting idea. "Hey! I just thought of something. That horse!"

"What's that?" said Head from inside the basket. "Is a horse coming?"

"The flying horse. Don't you remember it?" Barnaby jumped to his feet.

Babette sat up. "The mechanical Pegasus."

"Barnaby, you're a genius," said Bridget. She clapped her hands. "Hephaestus said it was almost done."

"It looked big enough to carry all of us," said Barnaby. "We could fly there!"

The kids gathered around the basket.

"Head?" Barnaby knelt beside the basket. "Do you think your master would lend us the flying horse?"

"I sincerely doubt it. Why should he? Lend it to mere mortals? Most unlikely."

"Would you mind asking him for us?"

"Are you mad? I would not dream of it!"

The kids withdrew to a nearby tree. They put their heads together and whispered.

"What is going on?" Head cried. "Return me to my master at once!"

A moment later, Head felt herself picked up. Her basket rose, swung wildly one way and another, rushed through the air, and finally came to a rest.

"Help! Help! What's happening? Help!" Head heard footsteps retreating. "Look here, if you have put me in a tree, I think it a very poor joke." In hopes the footsteps would return, she listened carefully.

They did not. Head heard nothing but the wind. It caused the tree limb that held her basket to sway in a way she found most disagreeable.

"Help! Help!"

No one answered. The tree creaked. The limb swayed.

"Help! Anyone! I am Head, the very valuable servant of the god Hephaestus! Help! Anyone who returns me will be rewarded! Help!"

Head listened. Nothing. The wind blew. Insects whirred. Birds chirped.

"Help! Help! Please, anyone, help!"

Nothing.

Head sighed. She clicked her lips together. "Oh, all right. If you get me down, I will ask Hephaestus to lend you the horse."

"Thank you, Head," Beauregard called. He and the others were not far away. "We knew you'd come around eventually."

"Even if you do lack a heart," Bridget whispered.

Head waited. "Well?"

"One more thing," said Barnaby.

"Yeah, one more thing," agreed Bridget.

"We need a guide to show us the way," said Babette.

"Never!" yelled Head. "Are you mad? You expect me to fly? Never! No matter how you torment me! Never! Do not imagine that I jest."

The kids and Beauregard walked away from the tree.

"This is most unfair! It isn't right!"

The kids sat down beside the road and waited.

Head groaned. "Oh, all right. I will guide you. But if you drop me into the ocean, I will curse you and all your descendants!"

The kids carried Head back to Hephaestus's cave. The whole way, they heard her muttering bitterly about her fate. "It's a pity," murmured Babette, "we do not have a sound-proof basket."

"Or a gag!" whispered Bridget.

When they arrived at the cave, they set Head on top of one of the three-legged tables. Except for the table, no one was in sight. Clouds of smoke drifted from the mouth of the cave. They could hear distant hammering.

"Take me to the master!" Head commanded.

The table rolled obediently into the cave.

The kids waited.

"Do you hear anything?" Beauregard asked.

"The hammering," said Bridget.

"What hammering?" asked Babette.

"That's what I mean," said Bridget. "It's stopped." All of them peered into the gloomy cave.

"She must be asking Hephaestus," Babette said.

Beauregard sat down in the tall grass.

"I wish we could overhear what Head's saying to him," Barnaby said. "Do you think we could just walk into the cave?" He took off his glasses, which had grown a bit smeary, and cleaned them on his shirt tail.

"We better not," said Babette. "When one asks a god for a favor, it is not wise to take his hospitality for granted."

Bridget rubbed the back of her neck. "We should have brought Hephaestus a present or something, some flowers maybe."

"Or offered a libation," said Babette.

"A what?" Bridget put her hands over her eyes and squinted into the dark interior of the cave but could see nothing.

"A libation," repeated Babette. "The gods are fond of two things: sacrifices and libations."

Barnaby raised an eyebrow. "Animal sacrifices?" He put his glasses back on.

"Ick!" exclaimed Bridget. She was very fond of animals and did not at all approve of sacrifices.

"I am afraid so," said Babette. "Sheep, goats, rams, bulls. The priests would kill them and offer their blood to the gods. I think they kept all the meat for themselves."

"Blood! Yuck!" Bridget made a face. "You said the gods liked two things. Sacrifices and—"

"Libations. You take a goblet, a very clean one made of gold if you have one. You fill it with wine and pour it upon the ground."

"Pour it on the ground?" Bridget looked shocked. "What a waste of good wine! Not that I really like wine; I prefer soda. But my mom likes it."

"All I know is the gods appreciate it when a person is willing to give something up, something truly valuable, I mean." Babette paused. "Maybe they feel we place too much value on our possessions."

"Babette," asked Barnaby, "do you think it would do any good if we gave up something? After all, we are asking Hephaestus for quite a lot. That golden horse is a fabulous invention. There's nothing else like it in the world. And we're asking him to lend it to us for nothing."

"But what have we to give?" asked Babette.

Barnaby commanded, "Everyone empty your pockets!"

A minute later, they gazed at their small pile: two pencils, one ink pen, half of an eraser, a piece of chalk, the guide book, a candy wrapper, a subway token, a small pocketknife, a wrinkled baseball card, two quarters, and one penny.

"It's not very impressive, is it?" Barnaby admitted. "This is all we have? No one's holding back?"

Bridget squirmed slightly.

"Hand it over, Bridget," Barnaby demanded, "whatever it is!"

Bridget dug deeply into her pocket one more time, "It's not fair."

"Come on, Bridget, what've you got?"

Bridget pulled out a piece of bubble gum.

"I thought you were out," Barnaby said. "You told us you chewed your last piece yesterday."

Bridget pouted. "Well, what's wrong with holding onto your very last piece? I was saving it for a special occasion." Bridget did love bubble gum. The others knew it. "I had to give up my Reggie Jackson home run ball just to come here. It isn't fair! What are you guys giving up?"

"She's got a point," admitted Barnaby. He reached up and snatched off his glasses.

"Barnaby!" Bridget knew Barnaby could hardly see without his glasses. "You can't!"

He tossed them onto the pile.

Babette reached up and removed her retro sunglasses. In the entire time they'd known her, Bridget and Barnaby had hardly ever seen Babette without her cool sunglasses. Babette tossed them onto the pile.

"Do we," Bridget said, "you know—burn them all up?"

"I can't believe we are really going to do this," Barnaby said.

They all looked at the pile of their possessions. "It really is hard to sacrifice things you value," Bridget said.

"Hey!" Beauregard exclaimed. "Someone's coming!"

"Is it Head?" asked Bridget.

"Is it Hephaestus?" said Barnaby.

It was one of the golden women that Hephaestus employed as helpers. The mechanical woman strolled toward them. "The master has sent me to ask you a question."

"What is it?" Babette made a polite gesture. "Whatever it is, we will do our best to answer the question." The others looked at Babette, wondering what they could possibly know that would be news to a god.

"My master hopes you can explain what has happened to Head."

"To Head?" asked Barnaby.

"Yes."

"Oh, no!" Babette slapped her forehead.

"Yes?" asked the golden woman.

"You opened the basket!" said Bridget.

"Yes, I opened it myself," said the golden woman.

"And Head looked at—?"

"Head was facing away from me; I lifted her out of the basket and, ever since, she has been—well, my master hopes you can explain her condition. Would you please accompany me? I will lead you to my master."

The golden woman led them into the cave.

They found Hephaestus standing beside the mechanical horse. Standing not far away, the tripod table still held the basket. Head was set on the table beside the basket.

"Oh, no," said Babette.

"I can't believe this," said Bridget.

Head was gazing lovingly at the mechanical horse.

"Ah, here you are," said Hephaestus. "Do you know what has happened to my poor Head?"

Babette explained what had happened at Aphrodite's temple. "We are terribly sorry, Hephaestus. It's all due to the fact that your wife put a spell on her. She fell in love with the first thing she saw. We thought Head would warn you before anyone opened her basket. She expected to fall in love with you, not the horse."

Barnaby cleared his throat. "Did she have time to deliver our message, sir?"

"Message?" asked the god. Hephaestus seemed rather pleased that Head had fallen in love with the horse and not him.

Barnaby elbowed Bridget. "You ask him, Bridget."

Bridget explained how they needed to go as quickly as possible to Demeter's Island. She left out the fact that they had promised not to warn Demeter or Persephone, not by word or deed, that Hades was coming. Amazingly enough, the god laughed and said he would help them.

"You see," explained Babette, "we did so hope you would lend us your marvelous horse, the mechanical Pegasus."

"Is he finished, sir?" asked Barnaby.

"Go ahead," said the god. "Jump on his back."

Barnaby leapt on top of the golden horse. It came alive! It trembled, its neck arched, and its eyes snapped open.

"Oh, how beautiful he is!" said Head, gazing at the horse. It was the first time she had spoken since the others had entered the cave. "I love him madly!" She glanced at Babette. "He's the strong, silent type, you know."

Hephaestus helped Babette, Bridget, and Beauregard mount the horse. Its back was so long, the horse easily carried all of them.

"Don't forget me!" cried Head, in a panic for fear she would be left behind.

The god dropped Head back into her basket and handed it up to Babette. He whispered into the horse's golden ear. Stepping back, Hephaestus smiled and said, "I have ordered him to fly you straight to Demeter's Island. Good luck!"

Hephaestus slapped the horse on his shiny flank.

The horse whirred as if an engine inside his belly had been turned on, shuddered slightly, turned his head toward the cave entrance, then began to walk. Its walk was a little stiff but otherwise very like the gait of a real horse.

"Be careful!" cried Head, sounding a bit overly protective.

The golden horse carried them out of the cave into the sunlight. His golden skin gleamed and flashed in the bright light. His metal hooves struck sparks as they hit against bits of gravel on the path.

Barnaby hopped down.

Hephaestus emerged from the cave. "What is it?"

Barnaby gestured at the pile of their possessions. "You see, to do you honor, sir, we were about to sacrifice these things. They aren't much but are all we have. " He blinked and squinted, not able to see very well without his glasses. "We are tremendously grateful for all you have done for us."

The god chuckled, bent down, and gathered up the pile of things. He gave Barnaby back his glasses, handed Babette her sunglasses. Bridget was overjoyed to get her last piece of bubble gum back.

"I deeply appreciate the honor you do me, but it is not necessary." Hephaestus winked at them. His ugly face crinkled into a smile. "Horse, do as I say. Carry them straight to Demeter's Island! Now fly!" He clapped his hands.

The horse ran forward a dozen steps, then sprang into the air, spreading its golden wings. The great wings caught the wind. They were airborne!

"Be careful, darling!" cried Head. "Watch out! Don't fly too high! Careful of that tree!"

With each down-stroke of his wings, the golden horse mounted higher and higher into the sky. The kids found it was a little difficult to concentrate on the view since Head shrieked so much.

"What I say," said Bridget, "is we put the lid back on her basket."

"Don't fly so high, dear!" Head yelled. "Remember Icarus. We're much too high!"

"I don't know why we brought her anyway," Bridget added. "Horse knows the way. Hephaestus told him to fly us straight to Demeter's Island. We don't really need a guide."

"Be careful, darling!" Head shrieked.

Babette looked into the basket. "Will you please quit yelling, Head? You are in no danger. If you don't, I will have to put the lid back on your basket."

"I probably shouldn't ask this," said Bridget, "but who's this ICK-a-rus she's shouting about?"

"I will answer that question," said Babette. "But first look—look at the view! It is so beautiful, so perfectly splendid."

The world of Greek mythology was spread out below them. It was a world of islands, of heaving ocean, of absolutely clear air. It seemed possible to see for hundreds of miles in that sparkling, smog-free sky. Far below, they could see dolphins frolicking in the sea.

"Some people say that dolphins are the origin of the mermaid myth," said Beauregard.

"Hey, did you see that?" said Barnaby. "That was no dolphin. That was a real mermaid! And there's another!"

"Horse, my love!" cried Head from within her basket, "don't fly so high! It's terribly dangerous to fly too high. Remember Icarus!"

"There she goes again," said Bridget. "Who's Icarus?"

"He was the son of Daedalus." She pronounced it DED-uh-lus. "Do you want to hear his story? It will help us pass the time as we fly."

"Is it a good story?" asked Bridget.

"It is an excellent story"—Babette smiled crookedly—"but I do not know if you will like it. The story of Icarus is one of those cautionary tales about how children should obey their parents, about how there have to be limits. In my experience, you Americans do not normally like such stories."

"Well, go on and tell it. Let us decide if it's a good story."

"Icarus was a boy, the son of a great man, a fabulous artist and builder named Daedalus. Except for the god Hephaestus, of course, Daedalus was the greatest artist of the mythical world. He built the famous Labyrinth, the maze that held the monster called the Minotaur."

"Oh, him I've heard of," said Bridget. "The Minotaur. He was like a bull. I mean, he was this really strong guy with the head of a bull. But I never heard of the other guy, Daedalus."

"Daedalus was employed by a powerful king, and one day he angered the king. As a result, the king imprisoned Daedalus in his own creation, the Labyrinth."

Bridget chuckled. "I don't think it would do much good to put a guy in his own creation. He must have been a pretty stupid king. I mean, if anyone would know how to pull off a jail break, it would be the guy who built the jail."

"That is true, and Daedalus did know how to escape from the Labyrinth. Unfortunately, the Labyrinth was on an island. The king made sure that no ship ever left any of his ports until it was carefully searched. Daedalus and Icarus could escape from the Labyrinth, but how could they escape the island? If they attempted to board a departing ship, the king's men would find them and return them to their prison. They would be severely punished for attempting to escape."

"So what'd they do?"

"Daedalus was indeed a great builder. He declared that even if the powerful king controlled the land and the sea, he certainly did not control the air. 'Look at the birds,' he told Icarus. 'They are free to come and go as they please.'

"Daedalus and Icarus began to collect feathers that dropped to the ground from sea birds. They collected both long and short ones. When they had collected a sufficient quantity of them, Daedalus built frames shaped like wings. He carefully attached the feathers, first the small ones, which he attached with wax; then the long ones, which he attached with strong black threads.

"I am afraid the boy Icarus was not of much help to his father. He played with the feathers and tipped over the pots of melted wax. Well, he was only a boy. Many times, Daedalus had to tell Icarus to sit down and be quiet.

"Finally, Daedalus finished the wings. He had made two pair, a very large pair for himself and a smaller pair for Icarus. He attached the large pair to his shoulders, then spread his arms. The wind caught the wings. He flew!

"The boy Icarus was thrilled, of course. He wanted immediately to climb into his own pair of wings and fly beside his father.

"Daedalus landed upon the ground and removed his wings. He told Icarus, 'I will teach you to fly, my boy, but please be careful. You must never fly too low. The dampness of the ocean will creep into your wings and make them too heavy to fly. You will be pulled into the sea and drown. Nor must you ever fly too high. If you do, the heat of the sun will melt the wax that holds the small feathers to the frame of your wings. The feathers will drop off, and you will plummet into the sea. Do you understand these warnings, Icarus?'

"The boy said, yes, of course he did. Icarus was eager to wear the wings and leap into the air. Daedalus carefully attached the wings to Icarus's arms and shoulders. He put on his own pair, spread his wings, and hovered in the air. 'Do you see how it is done?' The boy did as his father showed him. Soon, he too was hovering above the ground.

"One of the king's soldiers saw them and shouted a warning. More of the king's men came running. They had strict orders; neither Daedalus nor Icarus were ever to be allowed to leave the island. But by then, it was too late. Daedalus and Icarus caught the wind. They sailed up into the sky and flew away, free as birds.

"Looking up, sailors aboard a ship in the harbor saw the winged men and thought they must be gods. They fell down on their knees in fear. 'Shoot them down!' yelled the captain. But none of the sailors dared to move until Daedalus and Icarus were much too far away for an arrow to reach them.

"When they were out of sight of the island, the boy Icarus forgot to be afraid. He raced with his father, dived and swooped. 'Be careful!' yelled Daedalus. 'Remember my warning. Do not fly too low or too high!' And Icarus did remember the warning but not for long. Icarus flew high and then higher. He could not help flying high. It was thrilling to see the great sea spread below him. Well, you see how beautiful it is to see the waves flashing in the sunlight."

The others looked down at the sea and thought it really was one of the most beautiful sights they had ever seen. The sunlight caught the waves and made them sparkle like diamonds.

"Daedalus flew ahead. And then he called out to Icarus. But there was no answer. He looked back over his shoulder. Daedalus scanned the horizon from one end to the other, but nowhere did he see a sign of his son. Only then did he think to look down. There, floating on top of the waves, he saw feathers. Icarus had forgotten his father's warning. He had flown too high. The heat of the sun had melted the wax that attached the little wings to the frame. The wings had dropped off. The boy had flapped his arms but nothing could save him. Icarus plunged into the sea and drowned." Babette smiled wryly. "Well, you see, it is a sad story. Do you like it? As I said, it is not the sort of happy-ending story you Americans usually like."

Bridget wrinkled her nose and seemed to be about to defend her fellow Americans but, before she could, Beauregard said, "I don't like the looks of that cloud, do you, Barnaby?"

"Cloud?!" yelped Head. "What cloud?"

On the edge of the horizon was a small but very black cloud.

"We're flying straight toward it," said Beauregard.

"How do we get Horse to turn?" asked Barnaby.

"I don't know," said Beauregard. "Do you know?"

Barnaby shook his head. "There are no reins."

Babette whispered, "Are we in danger?"

"My master," said Head, "told Horse to fly us straight to Demeter's Island."

In the minute since they had first noticed it, the black cloud had grown noticeably larger.

"We are flying straight toward it," said Barnaby.

"Demeter's Island," said Head, "lies on the other side of that huge cloud. Horse is flying us right into a terrible storm!"

The wind began to blow briskly. The dark cloud grew larger. It swirled and pulsated as if it were alive and furious. It now occupied half of the entire horizon.

"Hold on!" Bridget yelled.

"Help!" cried Head. "Don't drop me. Hold me tight!"

But she had yelled too late. The wind caught the basket and sent it sailing into the air. Before anyone could react, the basket containing Head plummeted into the sea.

Chapter 7
The Island of the Sun

The golden horse flew directly into the storm. Hephaestus had told it to fly straight to Demeter's Island. No matter how the kids yelled and kicked and tugged at its golden mane, Horse paid no attention. It lowered its gorgeous head and flew into the storm, tacking one way, then the other. The rain engulfed them. Darkness swallowed them. There seemed no separation of air and water, sky and sea. The world was made of flying water. It was as if buckets of water were being poured over them, as if fire hoses were turned on them, hitting them from different directions. Lightning cracked. Thunder deafened them. The hand of the storm reached out, captured the horse by the neck, and gave it a shake. And just like that, Beauregard was gone. Lightning flashed and revealed that the spot where he had sat was now empty. Like Head, he had fallen into the raging sea.

Barnaby, Babette, and Bridget clung desperately to the golden horse. They hugged it with their arms and legs. It no longer tried to flap its wings but tacked wildly one way and another, more like a huge kite than anything alive. The wind blew so hard that the horse's joints creaked. Tiny, almost invisible cracks in its golden body produced eerie whistles as the wind rushed through them. The horse lurched abruptly. It was all Bridget could do not to fall. She swung her head to clear her eyes of rain water. Lightning lit up the sky for just a moment and, in that moment, Bridget realized she was all alone. Barnaby and Babette were gone. They too had fallen into the sea.

Then a curious thing happened. The deluge of rain ceased for a moment. The wind no longer pushed against her. But something odd was happening. What was it? At last, Bridget realized what was strange. She no longer clutched the golden horse. Bridget plummeted through the darkness. She no more than realized she was falling into the sea than she hit the water's surface and plunged beneath it.

At once, the world became calm, silent, and cold. Bridget could see nothing. She might as well have been locked in a safe on the darkest night of the year. Down through the silent water, she fell and fell. Curious thoughts came into her mind. She thought of her last piece of chewing gum. She thought of a boy with whom she had once shared a hot dog at Yankee Stadium. She thought of her mother's face bending over her.

And then Bridget thought of nothing at all.

When Bridget next opened her eyes, she found herself floating atop the sea. It was morning. An entire night had passed. The sky was pink; the sun was just above the horizon. The muddiness of the water and the fact that great masses of seaweed, torn up from the bottom, floated on all sides of her were the only evidence that a storm had passed. Bridget heard the murmur of voices speaking an unknown language. They were soft, gentle voices. Bridget wondered if she was asleep, experiencing a dream. Invisible hands seemed to hold her up. Perhaps she was dead.

"Ah, you are awake," said a soothing voice right beside her ear.

Not half a foot from her floated a head, very beautiful, with gray eyes and green hair that streamed in the water like seaweed. On the other side of Bridget bobbed another green-haired head, as beautiful as the first. What were they? Angels? Mermaids? The two beautiful women held her up.

Each time she began to sink, they returned her to the surface with gentle prods of their fingers.

Green hair? Bridget thought. I'm dreaming; I must be.

"Our master Poseidon sends his apologies," said one of the women. "The god of the Sea regrets bringing you harm. When he learned you are the ward of Hephaestus, he at once dispatched us to care for you."

"Poseidon?" murmured Bridget. She still felt as if she must be dreaming. "You saved me?"

"You are mortal," explained the sea nymph.

"And lack gills," said the other. "If we had not arrived to save you, well—" her shoulders, which were quite naked, shrugged prettily.

"The island is not far," said the first sea nymph. "Can you swim?"

"You've been blown far to the east by the storm, but here on this island you will find assistance."

Bridget turned in the water but could not see very far in any direction. A wave pushed her forward. She could hear the crashing of the surf. Her toes touched bottom. Before Bridget could even think to say good-bye, like seals slipping beneath the waves, the lovely nymphs disappeared into the sea.

Bridget waded toward the shore.

"Oh, maiden, we forgot to give you this. With Poseidon's compliments!"

Bridget looked back. One of the sea nymphs treaded water. A lovely arm emerged from the sea and tossed something toward Bridget. An object made of cloth landed with a splat in the water at her feet. When Bridget looked up, the nymph was gone. She looked down and found her New York Yankees baseball cap, so water-logged it floated submerged in the water like a half-dead jellyfish.

Bridget retrieved her cap and wrung out the sea water. She put the cap back on her head in her usual way, so its bill faced backward. Where was she? Some island apparently. Sea birds wheeled overhead. Bridget waded ashore. There was a beach, a big apron of sand. Behind that was a wall of trees. Exhausted, Bridget sank down at the foot of a sand dune.

"The pages of this guide book are stuck together," said a voice not too far away. "The sea water's totally ruined it."

Bridget sat up. That voice was familiar.

"I can't believe they returned my sunglasses," said another voice. "No one could have been more polite."

"What I don't get," said the first voice, "is how they knew we're friends of Hephaestus." It was a young man's voice.

"I can't imagine." That one was definitely a female voice.

Bridget crawled to the top of the sand dune and peeked over it. She saw two people talking. One was male and the other female. The male had hair that stuck out in all directions. The female was dressed entirely in black. In his hand, the male was holding the sodden remains of a book, not just any book, but the *Pocket Guide to Greek Mythology*.

"Barnaby?" whispered Bridget, hardly able to believe her eyes. "Babette?"

"Do you know what I think our rescuers are?" said the female. "Nereids. NEE-re-ids. Not mermaids. Nereids are one of the several types of water nymphs."

"Babette!" yelled Bridget. "Barnaby, it's me! Up here! I can't believe you guys are alive!"

The others shaded their eyes and squinted up at the top of the sand dune.

"Bridget?" said Babette.

"It is! It's Bridget!" yelled Barnaby.

Bridget ran, slipped, tumbled down the sand dune, so excited to see her friends all she could do was shriek.

Not until all of them embraced and laughed and wiped tears away did any of them mention Beauregard.

"You haven't seen him?" asked Babette. "Beauregard's not with you? We had so hoped you two were together and safe."

Bridget shook her head. "I just got ashore. I haven't seen a living soul except you guys."

Barnaby said, "You don't think—? I mean, if they saved us, the—what did you call them?"

"Nereids. Sea nymphs."

"Of course, they did!" declared Babette. She tried to look very confident.

"There's no doubt about it! We'll find Beauregard right over there—or there—or somewhere anyway!" yelled Bridget, trying to sound just as confident as Babette. But in fact Bridget was worried sick that she might never see Beauregard again.

"And what about Head?" said Barnaby. "She must have sunk straight to the bottom of the sea."

"She's made of gold, iron, and bronze," agreed Babette. "She's so heavy that I'm afraid . . ." she did not finish her sentence.

"My arms ached every time I carried her in that basket" said Bridget. "No way she could've floated."

Each of them bowed his or her head.

"Falling into the sea was exactly what Head feared most," said Babette. "That was why she didn't want to accompany us."

"Hello, there," cried a crisp voice. From out of the trees that fringed the beach rode a man on a horse. "I say, you are up early. Come to see Apollo drag her across the sky again, eh?" He waved energetically at the sun rising out of the sea in the distance. The red-orange orb was so enormous it seemed near enough to touch. The sun was so brilliant, they did not dare look at it for long.

"Apollo?" murmured Bridget. She remembered that Apollo was the god that Persephone was supposed to marry if only they could save her from having to marry Hades. Could this guy on the horse be Apollo himself?

The man rode right up to them. His horse's hooves threw up clouds of the soft sand. There was something peculiar about him, about his horse too. Bridget scratched her head. The man was immensely strong. He was naked from the waist up and bearded. His eyes flashed in the sunlight. A bow hung over his shoulder.

"Why, he's a Centaur!" exclaimed Babette.

That was it. Bridget hit herself in the forehead for being so slow to catch on. No wonder the "horse" looked so funny. It didn't have a horse's head. The man's body ended at the waist, where it was joined to the body and legs of a large horse. Bridget had seen statues of centaurs; she had seen them portrayed in cartoons and movies, but this was the first time she had seen a real one prancing in front of her. What a strange and magnificent creature! Mythology seemed to be full of creatures that were a mix of different animals. Mermaids were half fish, half human. Satyrs were goat below the waist, human above it. The famous Sphinx was a combination of three animals. It had a woman's head, a lion's body, and the wings of an eagle. There was even a fire-breathing monster called the Chimera that had a lion's head, a goat's body, and a serpent's tail.

"My name is Cressus," said the Centaur. "I've brought a consignment of arrows for Artemis and Apollo." He smiled in a self-satisfied sort of way. "We Centaurs make the best weapons in the world, you know."

"Artemis and Apollo?" asked Babette. "Can this be Delos—no, it must be—can we be upon the Island of the Sun?"

The Centaur looked at Babette as if she was a lunatic. "Of course, we are. What's the matter with you, woman? You don't even know where you are?" The Centaur snorted and trotted away from them. "Must be drunks!" He turned back to look at them once more, seemed to notice that all of them looked like people recently fished from the sea, and trotted back. "I say, do you people need any help?"

"We were blown here by a storm," Barnaby explained.

"In fact, we weren't sure where we were, not until you said this is the Island of the Sun," added Babette.

Bridget recalled that one of the Nereids had told her the storm had blown her to the east. Could this really be the Island of the Sun? From the Island of the Sun, each morning, just before dawn, Apollo harnessed his team of horses to the Sun's chariot. He struck them with his whip, yelled, and once more pulled the Sun up into the sky. Of course, the story struck Barnaby, the science whiz, as utter nonsense, but here in the World of Myth, it seemed literally true.

"The Palace of the Sun isn't far away," said the Centaur. He pointed out the direction they should take. "Apollo isn't there at the moment, of course. Won't be back till nightfall. But you might find Artemis. And the Four Seasons are always good for a chat." He waved good-bye and began to trot down the beach.

"Wait!" yelled Barnaby. "You haven't seen a cat, have you, a very large black cat?"

"A talking cat!" yelled Bridget. "Named Beauregard! Have you seen him?"

The Centaur paused and looked back at them. "Haven't seen any cats. Sorry!" He started to trot away again, then seemed to reconsider. Cressus wheeled around and trotted back to them. "Look here, perhaps I've forgotten my manners. Would you like a ride to the palace? You look as if you've had a pretty rough time of it."

"You can say that again!" said Bridget. "We fell out of the sky, nearly drowned, and—" Babette elbowed her.

"Thank you very much," said Babette, invariably the politest of the three. "We would greatly appreciate a ride to the temple. We've never visited this island before and don't know the way. And we are a little tired."

"Not to mention hungry!" added Bridget. Her stomach was growling.

"Come aboard then!" The Centaur reached down and tossed them one at a time up onto his back. He was immensely strong. None of the kids wanted to mention it, but he did smell as if he could use a good bath.

Cressus turned out to be nearly as talkative as Head. As he trotted toward the palace, he pointed out all the sights. "Never been here before, eh? Well, you'll like the palace. Marvelous construction. Built by Hephaestus. Fantastic. Hurts your eyes to look at it. Too bright by half maybe, but you know Apollo. God of the Sun and all that. You there—Babette?—don't know what you've got over your eyes—what do you call them? Sunglasses? They'll come in handy when you meet Apollo. Personally, I can't do more than glance at him. So bright he blinds you. Such a thing as being too bright, if you ask me. Have you met his twin sister?"

"Apollo's got a sister?" asked Bridget.

"Artemis, we call her. Remarkable goddess. One of my wife's favorites, to tell you the truth, though I've never met her. She dislikes men, that's what they say. Great hunter. Greatest in Olympus. Better archer than her brother. That's what I admire. I hunt a little myself. Artemis never misses with those arrows of hers. Was hoping to get in a little hunting here myself but it turns out the forest is restricted. Nobody's allowed to shoot in there except Apollo and Artemis. Was hoping to receive guest privileges, but so far no luck. Came here by ship. Got here yesterday. Didn't get a hero's welcome though. The goddess won't see me, and the sun-god is busy all day." Cressus gestured at the sun, which had climbed a considerable distance into the sky. "Of course, at night, Artemis keeps busy. Mistress of the Moon, you know. Loves the darkness, I guess. One hears stories. Her priestesses, out there in the moonlight, dancing and carrying on. No men allowed. No Centaurs either, for that matter. Here we are. It's right down there. Take a look! If that isn't splendid, you can call me a liar!"

The Palace of the Sun was indeed splendid. Entirely covered by gold, it glittered and blazed in the sunlight, bright as a bonfire.

"Told you it was bright. Squint your eyes if it blinds you. Come on. Down this way."

Cressus trotted along a path that wound its way down the hill, then trotted right up the steps of the palace.

"You seem very much at home," said Babette. She was a little surprised that Cressus seemed able to come and go as he pleased.

"The god of the Sun is known for his hospitality. Look around. Feast your eyes."

The roof of the palace was held up by columns. Each of them was sheathed in gold leaf and encrusted with precious stones. As Cressus trotted past a pair of columns, the kids spied rubies, diamonds, every imaginable variety of priceless gem. It was impossible to imagine the expense of each column. The richest oil sheik on earth could not possibly live amid so much luxury.

The two doors of the palace were made of silver. Each was at least thirty feet tall. Engraved on each of the doors were the Zodiac signs, six on one door, six on the other.

"Marvelous workmanship, eh?" said Cressus. "All done by the hand of Hephaestus."

"I've never seen anything so beautiful," murmured Babette. "But it is rather blinding." She adjusted her sunglasses.

"Wait till you see the inside!"

Cressus carried them through the palace doors, down a corridor and into the main hall of the palace. He helped them down, waved his arms. "Look around. This is the Great Hall. Empty now, it looks like. Artemis must be out hunting with her dogs. But when Phoebus is here"—he pronounced it FEE-bus—"the place swarms with attendants. Phoebus likes onlookers."

"Phoebus?" asked Barnaby.

"Phoebus," said Babette, "it's one of the names of Apollo. That's what they often call him, Phoebus Apollo. It means brilliant."

"He's brilliant all right," said Cressus. "God of healing, god of music. Look up there. That entire ceiling's made of ivory. Inspect the walls. You'll find the whole world there. All painted, of course. Every detail by the hand of Hephaestus."

The walls of the great hall were covered with painted images. Bridget, Babette, and Barnaby walked slowly around the room as if they were touring an art museum.

"You'll find all living things," said Cressus. "Animals, fish, birds. Look over there, the sea. Up there, the sky. There's mountains, islands, valleys, rivers."

"Look," Barnaby pointed at a section of one of the walls. Upon a painted rock in a painted sea sat a sea nymph, combing her long sea-green hair. "She looks exactly like the Nereid that saved me, Babette."

"Look here, Barnaby," Babette pointed at another painted rock, where three more sea nymphs sat. "Look at their expressions. They could be sisters." The Nereids resembled one another, yet each one was different, unique. They were painted so realistically it was almost possible to hear them speaking. The artistic skill of Hephaestus was nothing short of miraculous.

They found lions, tigers, and elephants. In the painted sea swam dolphins, whales, and sailfish. Hawks, eagles, ravens, and songbirds flew in the painted sky. Every species on earth was represented somewhere upon the walls of the great hall of the Palace of the Sun.

"It's as good as a fabulous natural history museum," said Barnaby. "I can't believe the detail!"

"My stomach's still growling," complained Bridget. "Come on, you guys. A person can get tired of even the coolest artwork eventually, especially when she hasn't had her breakfast!"

Cressus led them out of the great hall into another section of the palace, where its many lesser inhabitants lived. He found food for them, delicious fruit and freshly baked bread. The Centaur told them that, like all the other immortals, the god and goddess subsisted entirely on ambrosia and nectar, but everyone else in the palace ate normal food.

"When you're finished with the refreshments, come down this way. I want you to meet the Four Seasons."

The corridors around them swarmed with children. "The Days," Cressus explained. "There's 365 of them."

While they ate, Babette, Barnaby, and Bridget told Cressus of their quest to save Persephone.

"Do you think Artemis or Apollo might help us?" Babette asked. "We've lost the golden horse of Hephaestus and have no other means of transportation."

"Yeah," Bridget added, "we need a way to get to Demeter's Island."

"Can't say if Apollo and Artemis will help you or not. Gods are unpredictable. That's my experience. Now, Artemis does have a reputation for protecting young, unmarried girls like this here Persephone. On the other hand, it may be she doesn't want her brother married. Artemis the Virgin isn't in favor of marriage, generally speaking. She sticks to her hunting, she does, and has little use for men. But who knows? She might help if you were to explain how you want to save an endangered girl. That's the angle I'd take if I was you."

"But Persephone's supposed to marry Apollo," said Barnaby. "The god of the Sun will help us, won't he? I mean, he can't want Hades to run off with her!"

Cressus looked a little uncomfortable.

"What is it?" asked Bridget. "You're acting kind of funny."

"I can't say what Apollo wants or doesn't want. He doesn't confide in me. That's for sure. But I never thought of him as the marrying kind either. He's more the love 'em and leave 'em type."

The kids finished their breakfasts, quite surprised to hear Apollo described in this way.

"Come on," said Cressus, "this way. I want you to meet the Four Seasons. Why don't you ask them for advice?"

The Centaur led them down a corridor into an open-air courtyard that was just as splendid as the one they'd seen in the middle of Aphrodite's temple.

"There they are!" Cressus waved to attract the attention of four figures standing beside a clear blue pool, talking to someone.

As they approached, they heard a loud, high-pitched voice. "My beloved was torn from me, lost at sea. Yes, he loved me deeply. I shall never love another. No, do not try to console me. I must live in grief forever. Yes, he's lost forever I fear, taken by a terrible storm."

"Head?" said Bridget. "It can't be."

It was indeed Head. Their golden guide was not in her basket but was set on top of a low table beside the reflecting pool. Ranged around her were the Four Seasons. Spring and Summer were female; Autumn and Winter were male. Spring was a very pretty girl with flowers in her hair. Summer was a mature woman. In her hair, she wore a garland made of ripened stalks of wheat all woven together. Autumn was a black-bearded man, quite handsome. Winter was an old man with a white beard stiff with frost.

When she saw Babette, Barnaby, and Bridget, Head shrieked excitedly. "Where is he? Where is my beloved? Bring him forth!" Her eyes clicked back and forth, looking for the golden horse. "Darling? Where are you? You haven't left him outside the palace, have you?"

The kids were forced to tell her that they had not seen a sign of Horse since the storm had flung them into the sea.

"And how about Beauregard?" asked Bridget. "Have you seen him, Head?"

Head declared that she had not seen Beauregard since her unfortunate fall.

"But what happened to you?" wondered Barnaby. "Did the sea nymphs save you? They saved us! And somehow they knew we're friends of Hephaestus."

With great satisfaction, since she loved to be the center of attention, Head described her amazing adventure since a strong gust of wind had sent her tumbling from her perch upon Horse's back.

"I won't blame you, none of you, though you could have held me a little more tightly. I won't blame any of you, though

I might if I were a little less generous."

The kids did not say anything, though all of them doubted that if it would have mattered if they'd tightly clutched Head's basket, since the storm had grown so overpowering, it had eventually sent all of them tumbling into the sea.

"Unbeknownst to all of us, the storm was caused by Poseidon."

"The god of the Sea, you mean?" asked Barnaby.

"He enjoys storms, you know. Oh my, yes! He loves wind, rain, and cyclones. Nothing makes him happier. Of course, Poseidon had no idea we were on our way to Demeter's Island. He was simply enjoying himself."

The kids did not say anything in response to this revelation either, though all of them thought that in the World of Greek Mythology it often seemed as if the gods did pretty much as they pleased without any regard for nearby human beings.

"I fell and fell and fell, first through air and then through sea water, until I collided, quite unwittingly of course, with the head."

"Whose head?" asked Bridget, a little confused.

"You collided with Poseidon's head!" exclaimed Babette. She covered her mouth so as not to laugh.

"Very likely, for my impertinence the Father of the Sea would have fed me to a shark, except I informed him that I am the property of Hephaestus, a god whom Poseidon particularly admires. My master makes Poseidon's tridents, you know, and you may be sure Poseidon is very particular about his tridents. Besides, my master constructed Poseidon's undersea palace and his chariot and who knows what else? I let Poseidon know that my master's latest invention is my beloved! Oh, I miss him so!" Head paused, so overcome with emotion that for a few moments all she could do was click her eyes open and shut and would doubtless have produced tears if only she had been capable of doing so. "I let his

Majesty know that my master's golden horse, as well as three mortals and their cat, could all fall into the sea and drown unless he caused the storm to cease at once."

The kids gazed at one another, hardly able to believe all this could have happened beneath the waves while they were being knocked every which way by the storm's gale force winds.

"But," said Babette, "we did fall into the sea. All of us did. We nearly drowned."

"You would certainly have drowned," agreed Head, "except for my wisdom. Fortunately for you, I suggested to Poseidon that he rescue you, since you are all very good friends of my master. As a result, Poseidon calmed the seas and dispatched a half dozen Nereids—"

"There, you see," murmured Babette, "I thought they were Nereids."

"—to save you, all of you. I was carried by another Nereid, a very sweet girl, to this island, where I was discovered by dear Spring here and carried into the palace."

It turned out that Head's extended dip in sea water had caused some of her inner parts to rust. Not until she had been thoroughly cleaned by Spring's friends, Summer and Autumn, had she entirely regained her power of speech. "I was in the midst of telling them my story, when here came all of you. It is delightful to know you survived. But what about my beloved; are you sure you have not seen him?"

They shook their heads sadly.

"And what about Beauregard?" said Bridget. "Maybe your friends have seen him?"

Bridget described Beauregard, but the Four Seasons said that they had not seen him.

Advised by the Seasons that there was no way for them to leave the island unless granted permission to do so by Apollo or Artemis, the kids spent the rest of the day strolling around the grounds of the palace. Spring, the youngest of the Seasons, acted as their tour guide.

"Be careful never to go into those woods," the pretty girl said. "Those are Artemis's private woods. You especially, Barnaby. No male is permitted to trespass there."

Barnaby did not say anything, but he thought he did not much care for this goddess who disliked men. Although he had never devoted much thought to gods and goddesses, he thought the Greek variety pretty weird. The Greek deities seemed so nutty and stuck-up that he simply did not see how they were any better than normal people. So far as he was concerned, they were just one great big dysfunctional family. Barnaby decided that, if he and the others did not find a way to leave the island before nightfall, he would wait until everyone was asleep, then sneak out of the palace. He had a hankering to explore Artemis's private woods. People said Artemis was Mistress of the Moon, didn't they? She'd be occupied all night. The man-hating goddess would never know a male had trespassed in her private woods. Barnaby wondered if he might even find Beauregard and Horse in those woods. He smiled to himself, thinking of how surprised Babette and Bridget would be if they woke up next morning and found him sitting astride Horse, with Beauregard right beside him!

That evening, Barnaby, Bridget, and Babette had dinner in a small private dining room of the palace. Head was set in the middle of the table like a centerpiece. Perhaps because her mouth was not occupied with chewing, Head talked a great deal.

"Apollo will return this evening. I shouldn't be at all surprised if we are granted an audience. We will ask for his help, of course. Naturally, none of us have ascertained his views. Still, Apollo is the god of truth and prophecy. And healing. Are any of you hurt at all? He's very handsome. Some say Apollo is definitely the handsomest of all the gods.

I would like to see him at least once just to see if he is really as good-looking as people say."

Bridget wondered if Apollo could possibly be as handsome as Robert Redford or Paul Newman. Bridget liked modern movie stars like Denzel Washington and Brad Pitt, but she harbored a secret crush on some of the old stars. Her mother liked to rent old movies, so Bridget had grown up watching Robert Redford and Paul Newman. She thought them almost dreamily good-looking. If Apollo was even half as handsome as the young Robert Redford had been, he would really be something to see.

"Very likely," continued Head, "when Apollo hears that his intended—what is her name? Persephone?—when he hears she is in jeopardy of being kidnapped by Hades, he will at once leap into action. Persephone will be saved, the two of them will be wed, and we may all go home, our quest concluded." Head snapped her lips together thoughtfully. "I for one will be tremendously glad to go home. I have not had a minute's peace since I left my master's cave."

"Hey, Head," said Bridget, "I keep hearing about the glorious Apollo, but what about his sister? How come I don't hear much about her? Artemis is Apollo's twin, isn't she? What's her story?"

Head's eyes clicked as they rotated toward Bridget. "Artemis is beautiful, in a way. Of course, I've not yet seen her, but so people say. She is more like a boy than a mature woman. The goddess is slim-hipped, muscular. She dislikes court life, preferring the outdoors. It is said she prefers the company of her dogs to that of most people. Can you imagine?" Head laughed. "All she does every day is run around the woods with those dogs, or else with her entourage of maidens. A most unusual goddess, if you ask me, one that does not care for men. She's quite a good hunter, I gather."

Both Babette and Bridget rather liked the description of Artemis. She sounded like a goddess that a modern woman could admire, a goddess who was strong and independent, a goddess who was a great hunter, a better archer than any man. Neither of them knew much about hunting, but they thought they'd definitely like to meet the Mistress of the Moon.

"What's that?" said Head.

They all heard a knock at the door.

"Who can that be?" Barnaby asked.

From the door came a gentle but insistent stream of raps.

"Well, go and see who it is!" said Bridget.

Barnaby jumped up and opened the door. He turned to the others. "It's Spring."

The pretty girl walked into the room. "He's back. Want to see something?" She smiled enticingly.

"Who's back?" asked Barnaby.

"My master, Phoebus Apollo."

The kids looked at one another, wondering if they could just see the sun-god without any invitation.

"Want to see his chariot and horses?" asked Spring. "Come on. I'll show you the way. But everyone must be very quiet. No one must see us."

"Well, sure, I guess so," said Barnaby. "But do you think there's any chance Apollo will talk to us tonight? We're sort of in a big hurry."

"If my master will talk to you, he will send for you. Come on! The chariot is wonderful. And the horses!" Spring's eyes leapt wide open. "Wait until you see them!"

As they walked to the sun-god's stables, Spring told them that when Apollo finished his daily trip across the sky with the Sun, he drove his chariot and horses onto a raft that floated on the river that ran around the edge of the earth and flowed all the way back to his island. In this manner, Apollo returned to his palace. He stabled the horses, then spent the night with his court. Like all the immortals, Apollo did not need any sleep.

Spring pushed opened the stable doors. "Be very quiet," she whispered. "And whatever you do, don't startle the horses!"

Apollo's chariot was an awesome creation. Like so many of the beautiful possessions of the Olympians, it had been constructed by Hephaestus. Except for its silver spokes, the chariot was entirely covered with gold. Even in the moonlit darkness of the stable, it glowed and seemed nearly alive. Along its seat, a line of diamonds glittered like stars.

Two things about the stable surprised Barnaby. It was free of straw. All other stables he had entered in his life had been strewn with straw. This one was swept clean. Its floor was earth packed so hard it was like cement. The second strange thing about the stable, which perhaps helped to explain why it was free of straw, was its smell. The stable did not reek of horse dung but of brimstone.

"Do you smell smoke?" whispered Bridget. She squeezed Barnaby's hand.

"The horses," whispered Spring. "There they are! Look at them! Aren't they magnificent?"

Apollo's horses were enormous in size. They were much taller and more powerful than any the kids had ever seen. Apollo's stallions were so big that, if a Clydesdale had stood beside one of them, it would have looked like a Shetland pony. The horses were white in color. Their ivory-colored tails and manes were long and thick. One of the stallions must have caught the scent of trespassers in the stable. Its ears twitched. Its great head swung around. Its eyes were enormous, black, and fringed with thick eyelashes. The horse's nostrils flared as if it snorted a warning. A puff of smoke shot out of each nostril!

"They are fire breathers," whispered Spring. "We'd better not go any closer."

For some reason, the sight of the fire-breathing stallions disturbed Barnaby. For the first time, he felt a little in awe of Apollo. What sort of being could control these immense and dangerous animals?

Very carefully, fearing to disturb the horses, Barnaby, Bridget, and Babette began to edge backward.

A sharp, frigid breeze entered the stable. It was so cold, it made them shiver and hug themselves.

"Oh oh," murmured Spring. "Now, we're in for it."

"You there!" cried an icy voice. "All of you! Leave those horses alone! Come out here!"

In the doorway of the stable stood an old man, dressed in a fur robe. His long white beard spilled down his chest. Even in the faint light, they could see the frost on the beard, the icicles on the old man's eyebrows.

"Winter," murmured Babette.

"We didn't mean to cause any harm, sir," Barnaby explained. "We only wanted to look at the horses."

"The master will deal with you later, Spring," said Winter. "The rest of you must follow me. Phoebus Apollo has commanded you to appear before him. Come at once. You do not want to keep him waiting."

Chapter 8
Apollo's Court

Barnaby walked rapidly down the hallway. On one side of him, the warm side, was Spring. On the other side of him, the cold side, was Old Man Winter. As they approached Apollo's great hall, something bothered Barnaby, something besides the fact that he was warm on one side and freezing on the other. Of course, it was a little scary to be called before the god Apollo when you had just been caught sneaking around in his stable. Something else bothered Barnaby. Winter's breath came out in white steamy puffs. Although old, Winter looked strong as an oak. Not until the doors of the great hall sprang open did Barnaby realize what bothered him. Then, confronted by the splendor of the sun-god's court, Barnaby had no time to think about it.

What bothered him was Winter. Old Man Winter already existed. According to the story Babette had told them back in Bridget's apartment when this whole crazy adventure had begun, the reason there was winter was because Hades kidnapped Persephone. While a captive in the underworld, she ate some pomegranate seeds. As a result, Persephone had to spend half of each year with Hades. That was when the earth grew cold; that was why we had winter. But none of that had happened. Hades had not yet kidnapped Persephone. Persephone had not yet eaten those pomegranate seeds. So how come Winter was standing there in front of the door, big and cold as life? How could Winter even exist?

But there was no time to think about this weird problem. The doors flew open. Winter and Spring hurried to get to their places at the front of the court. Barnaby, Bridget, and Babette took a step after them, looked around, and froze, not sure what they were supposed to do. This was definitely the kind of situation when a kid needs advice. Walking into Apollo's court was not like dropping in on your best friend. It was more like visiting the pope. Were you supposed to bow? Could you say anything? Maybe you were supposed to crawl up to the sun-god's throne on your knees.

Afterward, they all said it was like being in *The Wizard of Oz*. It was like the scene when Dorothy, the Cowardly Lion, the Tin Man, and the Scarecrow first go to see the Wizard. The great hall was now filled with people, if you could call them people. Apollo's subjects did not mill around like people at a party but stood in careful ranks on both sides of the diamond-studded throne. The center of the room, the attraction that grabbed the eye, was the purple-robed occupant of the throne. The sun-god's head blazed with fire. Just like the sun. You could not bear to look for long at that nimbus of light. It hurt your eyes. An orange-rimmed black spot burned into your vision so that, no matter where you looked, you saw the ghostly image of that fiery head.

Bridget, Babette, and Barnaby tiptoed toward the throne. They felt terribly self-conscious. Everyone stared at them. The 365 Days were ranked on both sides of Apollo. The Months, the Years, the Four Seasons, and the Twenty-Four Hours stood to his right and his left. All of them stared at the kids as if maybe they had dirty faces. Babette, Bridget, and Barnaby began to clutch at one another's elbows. They felt underdressed. They felt awkward and silly and too much like Dorothy and company.

Then a wonderful thing happened. Apollo made a slight motion with his hands, and the blaze around his head went out. The blinding rays of light simply vanished, as if a light bulb had been switched off. The kids could look upon Apollo's face without shielding their eyes. He was handsome. But the word handsome hardly gives any idea of the appearance of Phoebus Apollo. He was young and manly and beautiful. His hair was blond and radiant. It curled gently against his brow. His eyes were a deep and brilliant blue, as blue as the summer sky or the deep blue sea. His mouth was sensuous, his chin strong and youthful. Bridget ceased to wonder if the god of the Sun could possibly be as handsome as her favorite movie stars. He was more handsome. Apollo was health, youth, and strength incarnate. He was splendid and perfect. It seemed impossible that a god so handsome could harm them.

"Sir," blurted Bridget, "your Majesty"—she wasn't sure how to address Apollo—"we're here to help you, to help Persephone, I mean. You see—"

The Days, the Hours, and Months looked shocked that someone was speaking before Apollo had given his permission.

Bridget stammered to a halt. "S-sorry, sir."

"We know who you are," said Apollo, "and why you are here. Since your arrival, we have watched you. We observed your appearance in the Swamps of Lerna, your visit to the Cave of Hephaestus and the Temple of Aphrodite. We followed your flight on the golden horse. Each day, I cross the sky. My never-blinking eyes see all that occurs on earth."

"Then, then," stammered Bridget, "you already know why we are here?"

Apollo leaned forward. His expression grew stern. "Do mortals dare to tell gods what to do?"

Bridget did not know what to say. She looked back at Babette and Barnaby for help.

"Do you come to our world to tell Aphrodite, Apollo, Demeter, and Zeus what to do?" the god thundered. "Do mortals plan to alter the fate of gods?" Apollo sat back in his seat and smiled.

Old Man Winter snorted. Autumn laughed out loud. The Months began to titter. Then the Days, all of them, began to laugh helplessly. The hall rang with laughter.

The kids were shocked. They turned red. Had they made a mistake?

Apollo waved his hands. The laughter ceased as suddenly as it began.

"I see that your hearts are innocent. Know that I will not assist you to leave this island. You must find a way to fly away yourselves." Apollo made an abrupt motion with his hand. "Now, go!"

Apollo blazed with light. The kids stumbled back, afraid they would be burned.

"Go!"

They turned and ran from the courtroom, feeling all too much like Dorothy and her friends running from the thunderous voice and the blazing ball of fire that seems to be the Wizard.

In the doorway, Bridget paused. She was angry. She whirled around and stamped her foot. "Wait!" The Hours and Months looked astonished, as if they could hardly believe Bridget dared to yell at the god of the Sun. "We've lost one of our friends—Beauregard. Have you seen him?" She looked up and down the ranks of the assembled courtiers, at the Days and the Months. "Have any of you seen him?" She turned to stare defiantly at Apollo, though the blaze of light around his head made her eyes water. "You said that you can see everything. Have you seen my friend Beauregard?"

"He is alive," said the Sun. "That is all you need to know. Now, go!"

That night, Bridget and Babette lay on couches in the palace room they had been assigned to occupy. Head was set on the floor outside their door. Since she had no need of sleep, Head could stand guard. Barnaby was in the room directly across the hall from them. They thought he was probably already asleep. Barnaby was the sort of person who fell asleep ten seconds after his head hit the pillow.

"I can't sleep," said Bridget.

"I can't either," said Babette.

"Why won't Apollo help us? You'd think he'd want to help Persephone, the girl he's supposed to marry."

Babette yawned and rubbed her eyes. In fact, she was terribly tired. "He said that we must find a way to leave this island. At least we know we are free to leave."

"The horses!" exclaimed Bridget. She sat up on her couch. "Apollo said we must find a way to fly out of here!"

"Yes, but—"

"Babette, don't you get it? Apollo practically told us to take his horses!"

"Oh, no, dear Bridget." Babette sat up and hugged her knees. "I can see why you think such a thing, but really, no. We cannot possibly steal Apollo's horses."

"Not steal them. We'll just borrow them. We'll get Head and wake Barnaby. We'll sneak out to the stables—"

"Oh, sweet, brave Bridget! Have you never heard the story of Phaethon?" She said the strange name carefully: "FAY-thun." Despite her desire to stay awake, Babette had to cover her mouth to conceal another yawn. "Please, stay right where you are. If I tell you this story, I believe you will see why we cannot possibly take Apollo's horses."

"I don't see why not. How else can we fly out of here?"

"Just listen to my story," said Babette, "and you'll see why."

"Oh, all right then." Somewhat grumpily, Bridget folded her arms.

"Phaethon was Apollo's son. Although Apollo had not married Phaethon's mother, Phaethon was his true son. His mother told him so. And Phaethon believed it. He bragged to his friends, 'I'm the son of Phoebus Apollo.' But his friends only laughed at him. Well, naturally; if one of your friends told you he was the son of a god, wouldn't you laugh? To make Phaethon feel better, his mother begged Apollo to bring the boy here to this palace and show him the fire-breathing horses and the golden chariot."

Bridget frowned. "I hope this story is going to lead somewhere, because it sure is taking you awhile to tell it."

"The sun god brought Phaethon here. He showed him this palace. He took him to the stable and let him sit in the chariot. He even let Phaethon touch the neck of one of the fire-breathing horses. Apollo told him, 'Because you are my true son, I will grant you any wish. What one thing do you most desire? Whatever it is, I will give it to you.' Apollo had set aside his beams, so Phaethon could look him in the eye. 'I choose to do as you do, my father,' Phaethon said. 'I choose to ride in your chariot, to drive your horses. I choose to drag the Sun across the heavens!'" Babette gave Bridget a significant glance. "In a way, Phaethon was like you, Bridget. He thought he could borrow the fire-breathing horses."

"So what happened?"

"Ah, it is a sad story."

"Another cautionary tale, I bet." Bridget yawned. She too was getting pretty tired.

"Apollo begged Phaethon to reconsider. He told him his wish was much too dangerous to be granted. Phaethon could ask for anything else; Apollo would gladly obtain it for him. However, Phaethon insisted Apollo keep his word. If he could not drive the Sun's horses across the sky, he would not have anything. When Apollo saw he could not persuade his son to change his mind, he told him, 'You must hold the reins tightly. The horses are strong and almost wild. Only the firmest grip will keep them on the correct path. All day, you must hold tight to the reins. Never let the horses leave the path, not by so much as a hand's breadth. Or else they will sense their freedom, and you will lose all control of them.' Phaethon assured his father he would do as Apollo said."

Bridget declared, "This story is starting to sound like the one about Icarus, that kid who wore wings and flew too close to the sun. I'll bet Phaethon gets in trouble big time."

Babette smiled. "Just before it was time for the Sun to rise, Apollo hitched his team of fire-breathing horses to the chariot. He wound the reins tightly around his son's wrist and again begged Phaethon never to leave the correct track. The boy was eager to be off. At the right moment, Phaethon cracked his whip and the horses leapt into the sky.

"In the beginning, Phaethon did as he had been commanded. He held the reins as tightly as he could and kept to the track. But after an hour or so, he grew bored. Why not let the horses gallop a bit? He gazed down at the world far below and thought how much fun it would be to dive down and scare people. Maybe he could even scare his friends. Never again would he have an opportunity to drive this chariot. Why not have a little fun? His hands relaxed a little on the reins." She looked over at Bridget. Her friend had lay down on the couch again but was still listening.

"Feeling their freedom and realizing that a weak mortal and not their real master was driving the chariot, the horses leapt off the track. The sudden jerk snapped the reins from Phaethon's hands. He cried out in fear, but it was too late. The horses ran wild. They flew high and then higher. They plunged down toward the earth. The horses brought the Sun so close to the world that whole forests burst into flames. Rivers boiled dry in their banks. Geysers exploded out of the ground."

Bridget closed her eyes. "I get the message. I can quit thinking about borrowing Apollo's horses."

eus had to knock Phaethon out of the sky with a
thunderbolt," said Babette, "or else the runaway horses would

have set the whole world on fire. The poor boy fell to his death. Apollo flew to the chariot and gained control of the horses. Only by a terrific effort did he manage to drive them back to the correct path. But by then whole areas of the earth had been scorched. It is for that reason we have deserts."

She looked over at Bridget and saw her friend was sound asleep. Yes, it was obvious that borrowing Apollo's fire-breathing horses was out of the question. They would have to find some other way to leave the island. Babette lay down on her couch and closed her eyes. In a moment, she too was asleep.

The next morning, Babette awoke all at once from a troubling dream. She and the Four Seasons had been somewhere, a vague, shadowy sort of place. Everyone had been happy.

Summer danced with Autumn. Winter played a flute, while Spring sang a pretty song. Then, as sometimes happens in dreams, everything abruptly turned odd. Spring and Summer screamed. As if to save their companions, Summer and Spring stretched out their hands, but Autumn and Winter began to fade from sight. Nothing could save them. Autumn's arms vanished, then his legs. Winter's feet disappeared, then his hands, his forearms and elbows. Both of them continued to vanish until finally there was nothing left of them but their heads. Oh, the sad expressions in their eyes! The two heads, the white-bearded head of Winter and the black-bearded head of Autumn, hung in the air like two helium-filled balloons, then vanished, and Babette awoke.

Across the room, Bridget was sitting up on her couch. She too had a funny expression on her face.

Bridget wrinkled her nose. "I just had the weirdest dream."

"About the Four Seasons. We were flying high up in the air. I don't know how; we just seemed able to fly. Then, all of a sudden, Autumn and Winter—well, it was pretty weird."

"What happened? Tell me."

"They started to fall. Just those two guys, Autumn and Winter. Not Summer or Spring. Like something was pulling them down. Until we couldn't see them anymore. Like I said, it was weird."

Babette told Bridget about her own strange dream.

"What do you think our dreams mean?" Bridget asked. "Or are you one of those people who think dreams never mean a darn thing?"

"I don't know what they mean. But it does seem curious we both had more or less the same dream—Autumn and Winter disappearing."

Bridget scratched the back of her neck. "Of course, in a way, when you think about it, Babette, if we succeed, if we rescue Persephone and end winter like we plan, well, maybe those guys really will disappear."

"It's sort of creepy to think about," said Bridget. "Like we'd be almost, you know, murdering those guys or something."

"Perhaps we'd better see if Barnaby's awake," Babette said. She hoped the dreams did not really mean anything.

Babette and Bridget jumped up, did some morning stretching exercises, then went out into the hall. Babette paused to scoop up Head, then knocked on Barnaby's door.

"He hasn't stirred all night," Head assured them.

With one hand, Babette balanced Head on her hip and, with her other hand, knocked again on the door, a little harder this time.

"Hey, Barnaby, wake up!" cried Bridget. She pushed upon the door until it slowly opened.

Barnaby's couch was empty.

"I don't get it." Bridget gave Head a suspicious look. "Are you sure you didn't drop off or something? Maybe he went to get some breakfast."

"I certainly did not 'drop off,' as you put it. I've never slept a wink in my life. Only mortals sleep. The very idea of me sleeping is absurd. You may take my word, Barnaby did not come out his door. He must be hiding somewhere in this room."

Babette and Bridget gave the room a thorough search but found no trace of Barnaby.

"I wonder . . ." Babette walked over to an open window that looked out upon a slope of grass and flower beds that led to the woods nearby.

"That's Artemis's private woods," said Bridget. "Remember what Spring told us. Trespassers keep out! Especially guys!"

"Bridget, do you suppose—?" Babette leaned out the window and looked down.

Bridget leaned out too and looked where Babette was looking.

On the ground, in the dewy grass, were footprints, the kind of tracks that can only be made by a pair of tennis shoes.

"Oh, no," Babette whispered.

" 'Oh, no,' is right," agreed Bridget.

The footsteps led straight into the forbidden woods of Artemis the goddess.

Leaving Head in Barnaby's room, Bridget and Babette climbed out the window and followed the shoe prints. They found a trail winding between the trees. For a moment, they stood at the edge of the forest, gazing at the trail.

"Do you think he walked down this path?" Bridget was so nervous about entering Artemis's private woods, she reached into her pocket, took out her very last piece of bubble gum, and popped it into her mouth.

"Goddess Artemis," called Babette, "I know this is your woods, and that trespassing is forbidden, but you see, Barnaby is our friend. We beg your pardon, but we really must visit your forest." She looked at Bridget and shrugged.

"Come on," said Bridget. "Barnaby's got to be in here somewhere."

They followed the trail through the woods.

Soon, the trees grew so close together, it was impossible to see far in any direction. As if competing for sunlight, the slender trunks leapt into the air. Most of the way up their trunks, the branches had fallen off, leaving little stubs. Way up at the top of the trees, the remaining branches created a canopy of leaves so thick it was impossible to see the sky through it.

"How do we know that he came this way?" asked Bridget after awhile. "I mean, a person could get lost in here, especially in the dark."

They heard a sound, a sort of yelp. Babette assumed a fighting pose. Since she was an expert at karate, very little frightened her, even weird noises in the middle of the woods. They heard a second yelp and what sounded like a loud slap.

They tiptoed toward the sounds.

"Up there," whispered Babette.

"It can't be!" said Bridget.

High up in the air was a sort of bag made out of ropes. The bag was suspended from a thick tree limb. The bag bobbed up and down, twisted wildly one way, then back the other way. Something or someone was inside it.

"Ouch!" They heard another loud slap; the bag twisted rapidly in the air.

Bridget and Babette tiptoed closer until they could see a cloud of biting gnats surrounded the bag.

"Ouch!" Slap! The bag jerked and spun.

"Hello, Barnaby," said Babette.

"Hey, Barn?" Bridget yelled. "Need any insect repellent?"

The bag spun violently.

Bridget could not help herself. She laughed. Babette tried not to but found it impossible not to smile.

"Help! Help! Up here! Help!" The bag jerked and spun. "Get me down!"

"You poor thing," yelled Babette, "we'll get you down. Bridget, we'll have to climb up there."

Smiling diabolically, Bridget said, "Don't be in such a hurry. When are we ever going to have a better opportunity to teach Barnaby some manners?"

"Manners? These bugs are eating me alive! Get me down this minute!"

"For one thing," said Bridget, "I think Barn should agree to quit interrupting me when I talk. It's terribly rude."

"I agree! Don't worry! Please, get me down. I've been up here half the night! Please! I'll never interrupt you again."

"Good." Bridget seemed ready to come up with several more suggestions for ways Barnaby could improve himself when she took a backward step and caused something to snap under her foot.

"Hey!" she yelled.

A large net, spread out on the forest floor and camouflaged with dead leaves, closed around her, and dragged her straight up into the air. In a flash, Bridget was in exactly the same predicament as Barnaby.

"What the heck?" Bridget grabbed the ropes that held her; she twirled helplessly in the air. "Hey! Get me down! Help!"

The bag was a sort of snare; it was connected to a thick tree branch. Bridget had stepped upon some sort of trigger, releasing the branch, which had sprung up and dragged her and the net twenty feet into the air.

From the bag containing Barnaby came a loud hoot of satisfied laughter.

"I hope the gnats find you!" yelled Barnaby. "See how you like it!"

Babette looked from one bag to the other. Now, she'd have to save both her friends.

"Over here, Babette! Forget Barnaby!" Bridget yelled. "Get me down! I mean it! I'm getting dizzy up here!"

"Sorry, Bridget, but since Barnaby has been hanging in his bag for hours—"

"That's right—plus these gnats are killing me!" yelled Barnaby.

"—I will climb his tree first. Perhaps I can lower him to the ground."

Carefully watching where she stepped in case any more snares were hidden under the carpet of dead leaves on the forest floor, Babette walked up to the base of Barnaby's tree and began to consider how to climb it.

Thup! Thup! Thup!

It all happened so quickly that, for a moment, Babette could not understand what had happened to her. She could not move her arms and legs. She was pinned to the tree!

Thup!

The shaft of an arrow quivered like a tuning fork an inch from Babette's wrist. It pinned one of her blouse sleeves to the tree trunk. A second arrow pinned down her other sleeve and two more her pants legs. Babette was not scratched but could not move an inch in any direction. She was nailed to the tree by four arrows!

From out of the woods strolled a beautiful young woman, carrying a silver bow. A quiver of arrows hung at her back. She looked like Robin Hood. She was tall and slender, slim-hipped and long-limbed. Her hair was short and dark, pushed back. She looked as much like a boy as a woman.

Barnaby spun in his cage of ropes, looking down at their captor. Bridget bobbed up and down in her snare. "Wow," she whispered. Babette was still so stunned by what had just happened to her that all she could do was gasp. All three of them knew exactly who it was who strode up to look at them: Artemis the goddess! She was the goddess said to be the most ruthless, the most jealous of her privacy, the most dangerous of all the goddesses. She was the Olympian known as the Huntress. Should they apologize? Should they beg for their lives? Perhaps they should tell her of their quest. It was said Artemis was the protector of young innocent girls; perhaps she would spare Bridget and Babette.

The goddess folded her arms and stood for a moment at the foot of the tree that held Barnaby, looking up at her prisoner. Then, before any of them could say anything, she turned and whistled. It was a loud, piercing whistle.

From the trees behind Artemis walked a horse—a golden horse. And on the back of the horse sat an enormous black cat.

"Beauregard?" whispered Bridget.

Chapter 9
Sirens

Excitement. Relief. Confusion. Excitement because, well, how could they not be excited? First, two of them were dragged high up in the air by snares while the other one was nailed to a tree by arrows. Then the goddess Artemis appeared, bringing their lost friend Beauregard with her. The goddess leapt up into the trees and lowered Bridget and Barnaby safely to the ground. Then Artemis came down and yanked out the arrows pinning Babette's clothing to the tree. She performed this astonishing feat with her bare hands. Amazingly enough, considering her reputation for standoffishness as well as her well-known love of dogs, it seemed Artemis was the friend of Beauregard. She was actually helping them.

Besides excitement, the kids experienced intense relief and happiness because they were reunited with Beauregard. Until the moment Horse strolled into view with Beauregard sitting on his back, they had secretly feared they might never see their friend again. After all, the last time they had seen Beauregard, he had been plummeting through the air into the sea.

Babette, Barnaby, and Bridget felt confused, above all; they could not understand what was happening. Why was Artemis helping them? Why was she in such a supernatural hurry to get them back on top of Horse and off on their journey to Demeter's Island? Artemis's handmaidens, each one almost as tall and athletic as Artemis herself, ran out of the forest with a big picnic basket of provisions. The kids climbed aboard the golden horse. Barnaby held the basket. Horse spread its wings, leapt into the air.

"Hey!" Bridget caught a large, round object flung up to her at the last minute by one of the handmaidens. "Head?"

"This time," Head replied calmly, "please hold onto me with both hands."

They were aloft. Horse's huge wings beat steadily, taking them higher and higher into the air. It all seemed unbelievable, a strange but happy dream.

Not until the Island of the Sun was practically out of sight did Beauregard answer all their questions. After falling into the sea, he too was carried to the island by a Nereid, a very pleasant sea nymph, according to him, though her green hair was disconcerting and reminded him of a punk rock star he had once known in London. He did not at all enjoy his long soak in the ocean. Cats object to baths, and a bath in sea water was not a memory Beauregard would treasure. He waded ashore and sat in the sun atop a rock until thoroughly dry. As cats will, he cleaned himself thoroughly before doing another thing. When satisfied with the fluffy condition of his fur, he stretched, looked around, and was discovered by Artemis, who appeared to be thinking very seriously of shooting him. Fortunately, Beauregard spoke up, said good morning, and apologized for trespassing on Artemis's beach. "I did not then know it was Artemis herself, of course, but she soon let me know I was free to worship her." Gods and goddesses, in Beauregard's opinion, never suffered from excessive modesty. "They have a certain air, I find, as if they do not consort with riffraff." Beauregard begged Artemis to pardon him for trespassing on her island but, after all, what else could he do? He was marooned. In any case, they soon became fast friends. "Artemis is fond of cats, even more fond of cats than she is of those yelping dogs of hers. Then again, all people of taste seem to prefer cats."

In the course of their conversations, Beauregard informed Artemis that he was accompanying three young humans, the sort liable to get into serious trouble unless carefully supervised by an experienced worldly cat like himself. It turned out the goddess rather approved of mortals who do dangerous things. She had not met the mortals Beauregard described but would keep an eye out for them. "Artemis does not care for the indoor life and rarely visits the palace." The two of them spent the day hunting.

Beauregard obtained several delicious mice, and Artemis brought down a large buck. "She is a wonderful shot!" said Beauregard admiringly. Babette shuddered, remembering how close the goddess's arrows had come to her.

Artemis went away that night, continued Beauregard. "She supervises the moon, you know." She reappeared at dawn, leading Horse. Artemis had discovered the golden horse of Hephaestus wandering up and down the same beach where she had found Beauregard the previous day. Very likely, still hoping to obey his master's orders and carry them to Demeter's Island, Horse was looking for Babette, Bridget, and Barnaby.

Beauregard then told Artemis of their mission, how they had come here from a far away land to save Persephone, the daughter of Demeter, from Hades, the master of the underworld. Unfortunately, their quest had not seemed to enthuse the goddess. "She has very little interest in the wedding plans of the other gods and goddesses, you know, and seems to believe that only fools fall in love."

Bridget nodded violently. She had come to a very similar conclusion.

"Not until I told Artemis that, unless we save Persephone from Hades, Demeter will cause all the plants to die, did she perk up."

"What do you mean?" Barnaby twisted around to stare at Beauregard.

"Haven't you noticed?" Beauregard looked at Barnaby as if surprised he would ask such a question. "You don't mean to say that none of you have noticed—?" Beauregard looked at all of them in amazement.

"Noticed what, for pete's sake?" asked Bridget.

"Well, that is why the goddess helped us." Beauregard spread his paws. "Why do you suppose she was in such a hurry to help us on our way? Because of the disaster."

"What disaster?" demanded Barnaby.

"We haven't noticed any disaster." Bridget looked at Babette. "Have we?"

"No, we haven't," said Babette. "What are you talking about?"

"The flowers, of course."

Horse tacked slightly to the north. All of them held on tightly.

"What about them?" asked Barnaby.

"They never opened this morning."

"So? Use your head, Barnaby. None of the flowers opened. Not a one! Don't you understand what that means?"

The kids looked at one another.

"You must be kidding," whispered Barnaby. He turned pale.

"Oh, no," murmured Babette.

"I must have taken a stupid pill or something," said Bridget, "because I still don't get it."

"It's begun then?" Barnaby asked. "You're sure?"

"It isn't just the flowers," Beauregard explained. "It's the leaves too. When I looked closely at a leaf, I discovered it was turning brown at the very edges. Every leaf I looked at was starting to shrivel."

With the heel of her hand, Bridget smacked herself on the forehead. Finally, she'd solved the mystery. It was happening.

"All the plants? Every one of them?" The thought that all over the world each and every plant was starting to die was so awesome that Bridget did not know what to say. She swallowed. "We're too late?"

Beauregard wiggled his whiskers. "While we were on the Island of the Sun, Hades must have come to Demeter's Island."

"He must have kidnapped Persephone," Babette agreed, "and taken her with him to the underworld."

"Since then, Demeter has cursed the world," said Barnaby.

"First, the plants will die," Beauregard said, "then every animal and insect that eats plants will follow."

"Until," said Barnaby, "no one is alive."

"The entire world will die?" whispered Bridget.

Barnaby nodded.

Stunned and silent, the kids sat in a row on top of Horse. It seemed impossible. They were too late? Because they hadn't yet managed to think up a clever way to save Persephone from Hades, a worldwide ecological disaster was already in progress. They had experienced lots of adventures, but none like this one. Everything they did seemed to go wrong.

"What I recommend," said Head, "is you open that basket and see what Artemis has given you to eat. In my experience, you mortals are never so demoralized as when you are hungry. Are you gloomy? Then eat something. That's my advice." She clicked her lips together.

Perhaps it was good advice, because after they all ate something from the basket, which was full of fruit, bread, and some sort of delicious drink, they did begin to feel a little better.

Since he could float on top of the prevailing winds, Horse no longer had to flap his wings. Advancing steadily toward Demeter's Island, the golden horse simply tacked one way and then the other, as if he were a condor. The day was sunny and perfect. There was not a cloud in the sky. It seemed impossible to believe that the world was truly dying.

"Do you know," Babette adjusted her sunglasses, "Bridget and I had most peculiar dreams this morning."

"Hey, that's right, Barnaby," Bridget tapped him on the shoulder, "we were wondering if maybe you had a weird dream like ours. It was about the Seasons."

"You mean when I was hanging from the tree limb?" Barnaby asked.

"We thought maybe you had time to doze off a little. It was a dream about Winter."

"Bridget, maybe you can sleep when you're being eaten alive by biting gnats, but I sure can't."

Babette explained how she and Bridget had dreamed that Winter and Autumn were disappearing. "In a way, it seemed as if it was our fault. Do you understand? Because of our quest to save Persephone." Babette described the terribly sad eyes of Old Man Winter as he had faded away to nothing in her dream.

Barnaby snapped his fingers excitedly. "I have a theory about that. I don't mean them fading away exactly, but maybe they will disappear. Who knows? What is really illogical is the fact they exist at all. While I was trapped in Artemis's snare, I was thinking about that very problem. If all this stuff has not already happened, why do Winter and Autumn exist? I mean, there they are in Apollo's court, standing right beside Spring and Summer. It doesn't make any sense."

"That is sort of strange," said Bridget, "when you think about it. Winter isn't supposed to exist until after Zeus rules that Persephone has to live half the year with Hades. But he does exist. We met him!"

Babette asked, "How do you explain it, Barnaby?"

"Mythic time."

"Excuse me?"

"This place, this time, it doesn't really exist, not in the normal sense. It isn't in history. I mean it isn't like going back in time, not at all. It isn't like visiting the Middle Ages or something. This world exists outside of time."

Bridget looked confused.

"Time isn't real here. Normal time. That's why the usual laws of physics don't apply." Barnaby began to wave his hands excitedly and talk as fast as he could, using all sorts of mathematical terms to describe his concept of mythic time. He went on and on until Bridget's eyes glazed over. She had as little idea what he was talking about as she did when he lectured her about quantum mechanics. Babette seemed to enjoy the lecture, but Bridget found her mind wandering.

It was impossible to think about mythic time. Instead, she daydreamed. She thought about sports and bubble gum, about her parents. She thought about love. In a way, Bridget agreed with Artemis. Only fools fall in love. That was definitely so. Bridget thought of various girls she knew who'd fallen in love with some guy who was obviously a jerk. You could tell one of these girls, "Listen, that guy is the pits." It didn't matter. She loved the guy. It was sort of pitiful.

No wonder the ancient Greeks thought love was a naughty boy, Eros. Just for fun, just to amuse himself, Eros shot an arrow into you. Then you were in deep trouble. So long as Eros's love poison raced through your veins, you were crazy in love. Bridget looked down at Head. Poor Head was in love all right, and with a mechanical horse! Horse wasn't even alive. Horse couldn't speak; he was more or less a robot. It didn't matter to Head. She gazed longingly at the golden horse of Hephaestus and hoped to be his slave. All because of Aphrodite's spell! Artemis was right. Love was strictly for dopes.

But no more did Bridget decide love was no good than she thought of her parents. Her mother was a successful lawyer; her father was a prosperous plumber. They'd been d practically forever, and they still loved each other. Friday night, they went out on a date. Lots of times, I caught them holding hands.

Even the ancient Greeks believed there was a variety of love that never ended. While Bridget, Barnaby, and Babette had walked from the Swamps of Lerna to Hephaestus's cave, Beauregard had told them a wonderful story about love. It was a myth made up by a Greek playwright named Aristophanes and told in a book by a famous philosopher whose name was Plato. The book was called *The Symposium*. If she ever got back home, Bridget thought, she'd go to the library and check out that book.

According to Aristophanes, each human being once had four arms and four legs, four eyes and two noses. They were incredibly fast, strong, and happy. They looked a little like spiders, scurrying around on their multiple legs, but humans didn't care. They considered themselves magnificent and beautiful. They were stronger and faster than any other animal. They could run down deer, horses, even lions. Nothing was safe from them. They were so fast and strong that they became conceited. Finally, the four-legged, four-armed humans became so powerful that they began to think they were the most important beings on earth. They ceased to worship the gods. Why should they bother? They were at least as great as the Olympians. That's what they thought anyway. Zeus, the father of all the gods, decided to punish the humans. To teach them modesty, to teach them they were mere mortals, he divided every one of them in half. Zeus divided them just as you would halve an egg by cutting it down the middle with a string. Each four-legged, four-armed human became a pair of two-legged, two-armed humans. The navel possessed by all humans was the spot where they had once been joined.

Afterward, each human was really only half of a whole. He or she was lonely, doomed to spend his or her life searching for that missing half. It gave Bridget the chills to think that, somewhere in the world, everyone has a perfect other half. Her dad sometimes jokingly called her mother, "My better half." Maybe somewhere in New York City lived Bridget's other half, her perfect mate. It made her tingle all over to think about him. What if she never met him? What if she walked right past him on the street and never said hi? Which myth of love was the real one? Was love just an arrow that hit you in the heart and turned you into someone else's slave, or was it when you discovered your perfect other half? Bridget thought, if she ever found her perfect mate, he wouldn't be incredibly smart and amazingly handsome. He would be a normal guy with a good sense of humor and plenty of street smarts.

Then, for some reason, Bridget began to think about Hades, the god of the Dead. She had never really given Hades much thought. If he was the god of the Dead, he couldn't be much fun. Hades was probably old and gloomy and maybe even mean as a junior high school vice principal. (She had in mind a person named Mr. Kersenbrock.) But maybe Hades was secretly lonely in his world of shadows and sighs. Who wouldn't be lonely in a world like that? Maybe, when Eros fired his arrow into Hades' cold heart, it made the old god happy. Maybe, when Hades saw Persephone playing with her friends, she was the most beautiful being he'd ever seen. Maybe his cold heart melted when he saw her. In a way, Bridget felt sorry for lonely old Hades. It wasn't the god of the Dead's fault he was crazy in love. Of course, there was still no excuse for kidnapping an innocent girl and dragging her off to a gloomy palace.

Bridget continued to wonder about love while Barnaby continued to explain his theory about mythic time. "So what I think is that, maybe if we save Persephone, Winter and Autumn really will disappear. According to my theory, they will have to!" Barnaby seemed to have a lot more to say, but when he stopped to catch his breath, he was interrupted.

"If I were mortal," Head said loudly, "I would stop up my ears." Head snapped her lips together to produce an emphatic click. "I would do it immediately."

"Excuse me," Babette said, "what did you say, Head? It sounded as if you told us to stop up our ears."

Barnaby looked a little irritated. "Wait, I'm not done yet. There's more about mythic time I want to explain. It's really a great theory!"

"Half a loaf of bread remains in the basket," Head said. "Roll up small balls of bread and insert them in your ears. They will make excellent ear plugs. That is my advice. Not that you ever listen to me."

"But Head, why should we do such a thing?" Babette asked.

Bridget decided that, when Head had fallen into the ocean, the salt water must have corroded her brain. "Like we're gonna stick bread in our ears!" she scoffed.

"Do you see those rocks down there?" Head's eyes swiveled toward the sea below them.

Not far ahead, sticking out of the sea, were tall black rocks. The waves crashed against them, sending plumes of foam high up into the air.

"So what?" Bridget asked.

"That is where the Sirens sunbathe," Head explained. "But don't listen to me. Do exactly as you please."

"The who?"

"Oh, no!" cried Babette. "Those really are Sirens! Do as Head says. Cover your ears!" She clapped her hands over her ears.

On the rocks lolled three beautiful sea nymphs, combing out their long green hair. Very faintly, Barnaby and Bridget could hear them singing.

Barnaby told Bridget, "You better do what Babette says. I read about the Sirens in the guide book. Don't listen to them!" He too clapped his hands over his ears. "It's very dangerous. Cover your ears!"

Bridget felt her friends were getting a little ridiculous, but just to be safe, she put her fingers in her ears. To her, the word *siren* referred to one of those loud, wailing horns that cops have on their patrol cars. It did not mean a beautiful sea nymph. Nor did she see how she would ever come to any harm just listening to nymphs singing. Weren't sea nymphs supposed to be friendly? Experimentally, Bridget pulled one finger a little ways out of her left ear. Instantly, Bridget heard the song of the Sirens. It was lovely, haunting. They were singing about bubble gum! It seemed nuts. Bridget jammed her finger back into her ear.

Horse was now flying directly over the Sirens. Bridget could not help herself. She pulled out both fingers just a little. The song of the Sirens was beautiful beyond belief. Their voices were lovelier, purer than any Bridget had ever heard. If only Bridget would let go of Horse, they sang, if only she'd dive down into the sea, the Sirens would catch her and carry her to a perfect world under the waves where she would receive a lifetime supply of bubble gum. Bridget really did love bubble gum. And she'd chewed her last piece yesterday. People who didn't chew gum had no idea what

agony she went through when she didn't have a piece to chomp on.

"Don't listen, Bridget!" Barnaby gave her a sharp nudge with his knee.

Bridget put her fingers back into her ears. Barnaby could be so bossy sometimes. He didn't even like bubble gum.

When she was certain Barnaby wasn't watching, Bridget loosened her fingers again, just enough to hear the song of the Sirens. They no longer sang of bubble gum. If Bridget would just jump into the sea, they sang, the Sirens would carry her beneath the waves to an underwater city where she would meet her dream boy, her perfect other half. He waited for her now. All Bridget had to do was dive down into the waves. The Sirens would save her. Didn't she want to find her true love?

Bridget looked down at the waves. Maybe she should jump? Her fingers let go of Horse.

"Yowl! Yowl! Yowl!"

It was Beauregard. He had his head thrown back and was producing the most hideous and horrible cat yowls Bridget had ever heard. Beauregard kept it up until Horse had carried them well out of ear shot of the Sirens.

"You can cut it out," said Bridget. "For pete's sake, shut up already."

Not until he was sure she was firmly clutching Horse did Beauregard settle down. "The Sirens have lured plenty of sailors to their deaths. You're lucky I distracted you. If I hadn't made such a racket, all three of you would have been goners."

"All three of us?" Bridget looked at Barnaby, who had turned bright red, and then at Babette, who was squirming uncomfortably as if she was guilty about something. Maybe Bridget wasn't the only one who'd secretly listened to the seductive call of the Sirens.

"They said they'd give me a lifetime supply of bubble gum," Bridget said. She decided not to mention the dream boy. "What'd you hear, Barnaby?"

Barnaby lowered his head in embarrassment. "It was something about the Nobel Prize in Physics for my theory of mythic time."

"And all you had to do to win it was dive down into the sea?"

Barnaby nodded. "And I almost wanted to do it. That's the scary thing."

"I did too." Bridget poked Babette. "What about you, Babette?"

But Babette only smiled her mysterious Mona Lisa smile. No matter how often the others asked her, Babette never revealed what she'd heard the Sirens sing.

Horse tacked one way, then the other. They flew for two or three hours.

"Are we getting close to Demeter's Island?" asked Bridget. She was getting as bored as she sometimes did on long car trips with her parents.

"Demeter's Island," said Head, "is just over the horizon. I advise all of you to prepare for landing."

All of them strained their eyes, trying to be the first to spy the island. What would they find there? Were they too late?

Chapter 10
Demeter's Island

As they flew toward the island, Head gave them a lecture. "Demeter is called the Great Goddess. Personally, I prefer the goddess Hera, but there it is. Demeter ensures that flowers bloom, that sort of thing. Most of the time, Demeter is generous and sweet natured. Of course, you do not wish to anger her." For emphasis, Head rolled her eyes. "Let me repeat, you do not wish to anger Demeter. Ever."

Barnaby ignored Head and leaned forward, trying to make out the island's features. Much of it was hidden by mist. He wondered if they could be absolutely certain they were approaching the right island. There were so many islands out here dotting the sea.

"Anger her?" Babette asked. "How could we do that?"

"Be careful, darling!" Head cried to her beloved Horse, who had just lurched. Horse steadied himself. "Not too fast, dear. Don't strain your wings!" She gave the others a severe look, causing her eyeballs to click as they snapped back and forth in their sockets. "You tire him. You exhaust him. Horse was just lent to you, you know. Really, none of you display the slightest concern for his welfare." In a soothing voice, she told Horse, "Don't worry, dear. We'll drop them here and fly straight back to Hephaestus. Poor Horsie, sweetest Horsie, I'll see you get a good long rest." Head began to whisper to her beloved in what sounded like baby talk.

Bridget frowned. "Oh, for pete's sake, Head, don't change the subject. If there's a way to anger Demeter, we should know what it is. Is it easy to accidentally offend her?"

Head sighed. "I don't know why I bother to talk to any of you. One might as well try to give advice to a herd of donkeys."

"I see something," Barnaby yelled, "there! Isn't that a palace?"

At the top of the island, the mist parted and revealed a white, gleaming palace. The graceful building appeared for only a moment, then the mist closed around it again.

Intent upon telling her story, Head said, "There was once a king. Never mind his name. It is a name that deserves to be forgotten. He was the sort of mortal who did just as he pleased, like too many others I could mention. Not that it would do any good." Head sniffed loudly. "Needing timbers to construct a fleet of war ships, the king decided to cut down an entire forest. The fact that it was no ordinary forest, but a woods sacred to the goddess Demeter, made no difference to his plans. He needed timbers. He ordered his men to march into the sacred woods with axes."

"And did the men march into the woods?" asked Babette.

Barnaby strained forward as far as he could without actually toppling over. "Are you sure this is Demeter's Island? I can't see a single flower."

"Their leader was the first to raise his ax. He struck a mighty blow against one of the trees. The poor tree screamed."

"It what?!" Bridget looked skeptical. "Hard to believe a tree screamed."

"Bright red blood poured down its trunk," insisted Head.

"Oh, come on, a tree bled? You gotta be kidding me."

"All the men, including their leader, fled. They feared the wrath of Demeter, even if their king did not. When the king heard what had happened, he ordered the men back into the woods. He took up an ax himself. To show them that he was more mighty than Demeter, he chopped down the first tree himself. Each time the king's ax bit into its wood, the tree cried out, but the king would not cease until the tree fell to the ground. 'Take all of them,' he cried to his men. 'In the morning, I want to look out my window and see this entire forest leveled.'"

"Wow," Bridget said, "that's what they call clear cutting."

"We'll be over the island in a couple minutes," said Barnaby. "Maybe we should circle it first, just to see if this is the right place."

"The next morning, the king awoke and looked out his window. The forest was leveled. He called for his breakfast. 'You see,' he told his lords when they came to breakfast with him, 'the Great Goddess is afraid of me.' He ate a plate of eggs, then wiped his mouth. 'Do you know, I'm still hungry. Isn't that strange?' He called for a second helping. But even after consuming it, he was still hungry. The king consumed one plate of food after another, but he could not seem to get any nourishment. No matter how much food he ate, he continued to feel as if he hadn't eaten a thing."

"Was that Demeter's revenge?" asked Babette. "She made him insatiable?"

"That king was already insatiable. Demeter merely demonstrated the fact. It is said he did nothing but eat for thirty days and thirty nights. He devoured thousands of chickens, an entire herd of cattle, orchards of fruit, acres of vegetables. Nothing he ate gave him any satisfaction. His hunger grew and grew. At last, he starved to death, surrounded by food. That was Demeter's revenge."

"In a way," Babette said, "it's an ecological fable. Demeter is an environmentalist who doesn't approve of clear cutting."

"The mist is lifting!" Barnaby yelled.

"I'll tell you a little about this island," said Head. Once she began talking, it was her habit to continue whether very many people seemed to be listening or not. "Upon one side of the island, the northern side, it is perpetually spring. Upon the other side, the southern, it is perpetually summer. On the spring side, the air is fragrant with the scent of thousands of fresh flowers. Every variety in the world blooms there. They bloom constantly. No flower ever dies, or even withers. On the other side of the island, the summer side, the plants continually bear fruit. All year round, there are plums, pomegranates, oranges, grapes, figs, and olives."

"It sounds like the Garden of Eden," said Bridget.

"I know nothing of that garden," said Head, "but if it remotely resembles Demeter's Island, it must be a lovely place indeed. Because the island is the holy place of Demeter, nothing dies there. Nothing ages or decays. The priestesses who serve Demeter never grow old. They remain forever young, forever beautiful and happy. It is said, if a sick person is brought to Demeter's Island, she will grow well the moment her foot touches its fertile soil. If a mortal is old, she will grow young as soon as she tastes any of Demeter's fruit."

"I don't think this is it!" Barnaby yelled. "Horse must have taken a wrong turn!"

As the mist lifted, they saw the island directly below them. Horse slowly circled above it. What few flowers there were sprawled dead on the ground. The forests had dropped their leaves. The trees were bare and gnarled; their naked branches twisted into the sky. The smell that rose from the island was not of perfume or delicious fruit, but of rot and decay.

"I agree with Barnaby. We must be lost." Babette frowned with concern. "This island is nothing like the one Head just described."

Head snapped her lips. "This is Demeter's Island. Something terrible has occurred here."

"Then, where are all the priestesses?" asked Bridget. "Didn't you say Demeter's priestesses are forever young? I don't see anybody down there except old ladies."

Here and there, small groups of white-haired women huddled together. The kids could hear their wails of grief. Many of them stumbled as they walked. Their fingers blindly groped the air.

"It's like some sort of giant old-folks' home," said Bridget.

"Maybe we better check out that palace we saw," Barnaby said.

Horse flew to the top of the island and landed in front of the palace they had seen earlier. If the palace had seemed beautiful from a great distance, it did not look so great up close. Jagged cracks ran through its columns. Its steps were stained and broken. Everywhere, they saw signs of decay and neglect.

"I don't know who owns this place," Bridget said, "but she needs to hire a new maintenance man."

"Head," asked Babette, "are you certain we've come to the right place?"

"You stand before the Palace of Demeter," Head said.

A woman, wrapped in a tattered black cloak, appeared in the doorway of the palace. She was so old and feeble, she tottered on her feet. Her face was a mass of wrinkles.

"Oh, the poor thing," said Babette. "We'd better help her. She might fall." The steep flight of steps that ran up to the palace doors certainly did not seem handicapped-accessible.

Barnaby called out, "Ma'am? Could you please tell us if this is the palace of the goddess Demeter?"

"Could we help you down those steps?" asked Babette.

"All of you are to come at once," called the old woman. "My mistress awaits. I am commanded to lead you to her sanctum."

The kids exchanged looks. "What do you think, Beauregard?" asked Bridget.

"Please," called the ancient woman, "you must hurry. We have been waiting all morning for your arrival."

Beauregard wiggled his whiskers. "I guess we will never know for sure what happened here unless we follow her."

Beauregard and Babette led the others up the steps. "But how'd they know we were coming?" whispered Bridget.

"Shush!" hissed Head. "We are now entering the Palace of the Great Goddess. You must not speak unless spoken to!"

Bridget rather regretted that she had agreed to carry Head in her arms. They were already aching. Head weighed a ton!

As they walked through the corridors of the palace, they saw that room after room was in disarray. Furniture had fallen over and never been picked up. Litter and trash were everywhere. Where were the servants? The only people they saw were other old women like the one who led them deeper into the palace. Where were the eternally young priestesses that Head had described? In every room, ancient women sat on benches, wringing their hands and mumbling to themselves as if they'd lost their wits.

"Please, wait here," said the old woman, pointing to a small room containing several benches. "I will tell my mistress you have arrived." She went through a door, closing it carefully after her.

They waited, not speaking or even looking at one another. No one said it, but they all had the same thought. Wasn't all this their fault? If only they had gotten here sooner.

"My mistress will see you now," said a voice. It was the old woman. "Follow me."

The old woman led them into a large room containing a well that stank of sulfur. From its mouth rose tendrils of yellow and brown mist. Not far away, an area of the room was blocked off by a dark veil. Something or someone was hidden behind it, but they couldn't tell what it was.

"Mistress," called the old woman, "your guests are here." She bowed to the veil, then backed away from it, as one might back away from a queen. As she passed them, the old woman whispered, "The High Priestess will speak with you now. You must not speak first." The old woman left the room.

The High Priestess, Bridget thought. So it was not Demeter.

The door clicked as the old woman closed it behind her.

"Do you need anything?" asked a high, thin, cracked voice. "You have come a long distance from the Island of the Sun. If you are hungry, I will send for refreshments, though as you can see, my assistants no longer move so quickly as they once did."

They all stared at the veil. Beauregard lashed his long tail, while Barnaby wiggled his fingers.

"That is quite all right," said Babette. "We are not hungry. But thank you for asking."

"How do you know where we came from?" Bridget demanded. Then, remembering the fate of the king who had offended the goddess Demeter, she blurted, "No offense! I just wondered." Perhaps it was nearly as dangerous to offend Demeter's high priestess as to irritate the Great Goddess.

The veil rippled as if touched by a slight breeze.

"Are you the High Priestess?" asked Babette. "Let me introduce us. This is—"

"I know who you are," said the thin, cracked voice. "The cat is Beauregard. The young man is Barnaby. You, the one dressed in black, are Babette, and the other one, the one who asks impertinent questions, is Bridget."

"How does she know our names?" Bridget hissed, then popped her hand over her mouth. It was as if the person on the other side of the veil was a psychic. Bridget thought things like the Psychic Hotline were strictly for dopes, but still, it was a little creepy that this priestess knew their names. Could she really know why they were here?

"Please, pull back the veil," said the voice.

Babette and Barnaby stepped forward to draw it back.

"When you see me, gasp if you must. I will take no offense."

Babette and Barnaby looked at each other.

"Go ahead," the voice said, "I am ready now."

Slowly, Babette and Barnaby pulled back the veil.

On the other side of it was a high-backed throne. At its feet was a litter, and upon it lay an old woman. The word *old* hardly gives any idea of just how old the woman was. She was so frail, so thin, so pale and wrinkled that she hardly seemed alive. Her skin was thin as tissue paper; one could almost see through it. She looked hundreds of years old! The ancient high priestess hardly moved. Bridget had the idea that, if you gave the priestess a poke, she might break into pieces. That is how fragile she appeared.

The priestess hardly breathed. Only the fact that her eyes were open revealed she was truly alive. Large, feverish, and glowing, they carefully inspected Babette, Barnaby, Beauregard, and Bridget.

"What about me?" snapped Head. Bridget had set her on the floor soon after coming into the room. "Am I never to be introduced?"

"Head of Hephaestus, you need no introduction here," whispered the High Priestess. "I know who you are. Although you no longer recognize me, we have met before."

Head stared in surprise at the ancient woman, "High Priestess? Can it be you? But you were so young, so beautiful!"

"Please, come close. All of you. It tires me to talk, and to speak loudly. I know who you are, and why you are here. I have watched you approach on your golden horse. Come close. Kneel around me and do not interrupt."

Babette and Barnaby knelt beside the High Priestess's head. Beauregard and Bridget knelt at her side. Bridget slid Head forward until she was right beside the priestess' waist. She wondered how in the world this bedridden old lady could have watched them approach the island.

"I am the High Priestess of this temple. Only yesterday, I was young and beautiful. Only yesterday, I was the lovely girl that Head remembers." The priestess gasped. "No, I am all right. Just let me get my breath." She coughed, swallowed. "Disaster has befallen our island. Our precious is gone. Our treasure is stolen." Two bright spots of red appeared in her withered cheeks. "Look, look into the vapors and you will see all that has occurred here."

The kids turned to look at the well. Babette pointed at it. "It must be the Well of Demeter. I've read about it. The priestesses of Demeter gazed into the vapors that rose from it, then gave the oracle."

"Look there!" Barnaby cried. He pointed at the vapors issuing from the mouth of the well. "Don't you see them?"

Ghostly shapes appeared and disappeared inside the vapors; semitransparent forms flickered and danced, vanished, then reappeared. Bridget whispered, "Wow. It's like some weird kind of TV. It's like instant replay!"

In the vapors, they saw a flower-filled meadow. A dozen girls played there, dancing and frolicking, giggling wildly as they chased one another. All of them were lovely and vivacious, but one of them, with long black hair and dark flashing eyes, was especially beautiful. She seemed to be the leader of the girls. A garland of flowers was set atop her head like a crown. Her lips were bright red and inclined to smile. When she threw back her head, her long slender neck appeared, lovely as the neck of a vase.

"Persephone," whispered Babette. "It must be. She looks so happy."

"These are the events of yesterday," whispered the high priestess.

In the meadow, the girls suddenly stopped playing; they began to look wildly around them as if something terrible and mysterious was happening, something they could barely comprehend. A huge hole opened up in the meadow. Out of it galloped a team of black horses. Each one had a set of sharp fangs. Puffs of smoke shot out of their nostrils. These huge and terrifying animals pulled an ebony black chariot out of the hole and into the light.

In the well of the chariot stood a giant warrior dressed entirely in black armor. His face was hidden by a black helmet that bore a tall, black plume.

The moment, the horses leapt up out of the hole in the ground, the girls fled. All but one. The most beautiful of them, the one who had seemed their leader, stood her ground.

In the next few minutes, Bridget, Babette, and Barnaby saw what had happened in the meadow. It was the same sequence of events that Babette had described at the start of their adventure, when they were all gathered in Bridget's New York City apartment, but now these events did not seem like a mere story. They seemed horribly real. There really was a girl named Persephone. The earth really did shake violently. A giant warrior dressed all in black really did burst out of the ground, seize her to his chest, and fly off with her into the sky.

In the vapors that rose from the well they saw the gigantic hole close. Slowly and steadily, like a huge mouth shutting, it closed until it was no more. That was the oddest thing. After the hole sealed shut, the meadow seemed exactly as it was before. The sun continued to shine. A gentle breeze caused the flowers to bob and nod. A pretty butterfly flew from blossom to blossom as if nothing of any importance had happened.

In the next hour, the high priestess told them what had occurred after Persephone was taken captive by the mysterious warrior.

"When the Great Goddess learned what had occurred, that her beautiful Persephone had been stolen, her grief was beyond description. Her anger was more intense than her grief. She has left us. Demeter has gone to find Persephone. The Great Goddess has cursed the world. Nothing will grow. No flower will bloom until Demeter holds Persephone in her arms again. Never will she return to us, not until she finds her daughter."

"But what else has happened here? You and the others, you have become so—" Babette did not dare finish her sentence, did not dare to ask how they came to be so shockingly aged.

"While our island was blessed by the Great Goddess, no one aged. No one grew ill; no one ever died. But now the goddess has left us. We have become old all at once. Although I am 250 years old, until Demeter abandoned us, I seemed young as a girl. We all seemed young. Our goddess gave us health, beauty." The high priestess heaved a sigh. "Demeter no longer blesses us. You see, we failed her. We failed to protect Persephone."

Half an hour later, the kids and Beauregard stumbled out of the temple. They blinked their eyes, nearly blind, like people coming out of a dark movie theatre. It all seemed incredible. If they did not see the evidence all around them, the brown and dying plants, the aged women, they would never have believed it. Demeter had cursed the world. Nothing would grow until she found Persephone.

Before they left her, the high priestess asked for their help with what seemed a simple task. "Do you see that mirror there?" A small mirror, attached to a cord, lay at the priestess's side.

"It's cracked," said Bridget, picking it up carefully.

"It must be lowered into the well, lowered to the length of the cord. When you have done so, bring it back up. Carry it here to me. On its surface, I will discover what you must do now. Or have you abandoned your quest? Do you no longer wish to help Demeter, to save Persephone? Have you lost your courage?" The brilliant, feverish eyes of the priestess searched their faces. "No one will blame you if you have."

"Oh, no," Babette said. "I mean—" She looked at the others. "We haven't given up, have we?"

"No way," said Bridget.

"Barnaby? Beauregard?"

All of them swore to continue their quest.

"But how?" asked Barnaby. "What are we supposed to do now?"

"Lower the mirror into the well," whispered the priestess. Her aged hands moved in the air; they seemed delicate things made of glass. "Please, hurry. I have so little strength left."

Barnaby looked at the others, then carried the mirror to the well, peered down into it. All he could see was darkness. The well seemed to go down forever. It stank of sulfur. The vapor clouds made him choke. With one hand, Barnaby held his nose. With the other, he dropped the mirror into the well. He lowered it until he came to the end of the string.

"Bring it back up!" whispered Bridget.

Barnaby drew up the mirror until he held it in his hand.

"Bring it here. Hurry!" cried the old priestess. "I must see what is written on its surface."

Holding it by its edges, Barnaby carried the cracked mirror to the priestess.

Summoning up all her remaining strength, the old woman took hold of the mirror. She brought it to her eyes and inspected it carefully for a long time. At last she fell back, letting the mirror fall to the floor at her side.

"What is it? Are you all right?" Babette reached out and pushed back a strand of white hair from the priestess's forehead. The large eyes swiveled toward her.

"What did you see?" asked Barnaby.

"Tiresias," said the priestess, gazing at Babette. "I do not understand."

"What'd she say?" Barnaby asked. "Ty-what?"

"Ty-REE-see-uhs," whispered Babette slowly, "the most famous seer of the ancient world."

"You must go to Delphi," murmured the old woman. "There you must consult Tiresias. That is all I know." She closed her eyes and sighed deeply.

"Wow. Is she okay? She's not, you know—" Bridget made a helpless gesture.

"I think she's just fallen asleep," said Babette. They tiptoed out of the temple.

Now, they stood at the foot of the temple steps. Horse waited patiently not far away.

"Delphi!" snapped Head. "We are never going to get back home. Well, come on then. What are we waiting for?"

"One good thing," Bridget snapped her fingers and grinned. "At least we didn't have to break our vow. You know how we promised Aphrodite we wouldn't warn anyone here that Hades was coming to kidnap Persephone? Well, since he's already grabbed her, we don't have to worry about that one anymore."

"Horsie, darling," cried Head, "you will have to carry us all to Delphi. But please be careful. Don't strain yourself. These mortals aren't worth it!"

Barnaby helped the others climb aboard Horse, then swung himself up onto the golden horse's back. It seemed to him they were a long way from home. Who knew how this adventure was going to turn out? Now, they had to fly to Delphi. And see some crazy guy named Tiresias. Would they ever save Persephone? It didn't seem likely. And no matter what, how were they ever going to get back to the real world?

When all of them were in their places, Horse spread his wings, ran forward three steps, and leapt into the sky.

Chapter 11
The Pythoness

Perhaps it was the sea air, or perhaps it was the monotonous swaying of Horse as he flew through the sky. After an hour or so, they all felt a little seasick. Or perhaps it was just that they were tired. None of them had gotten much sleep. There are many good things to be said about exciting adventures, but they certainly are not restful. Whatever the reason, all of them fell into a bad mood. Pretty soon, they were arguing.

Barnaby began the argument by saying it was stupid to care what Demeter's high priestess had said. It was ridiculous to believe in fortune tellers. No sane person would pay a fortune teller a dime. Besides, this particular priestess was 250 years old. "She was sickly and probably senile. Right? I wouldn't be surprised if she was suffering from Alzheimer's. She's sent us on a wild goose chase."

Bridget did not help matters. When they had fallen into the sea, the guide book Barnaby had brought had gotten so water-logged, it had seemed utterly ruined. But Bridget had saved it. She'd set it out in the sun and let the pages dry out. When they'd flown to Demeter's Island, she'd brought it with her. Now, having nothing better to do, she pried apart its pages. After reading for awhile, she wrinkled her forehead. "One thing bothers me, Babette. When you first told us the story of Persephone didn't you say that the god Hades came out of the hole in the ground, grabbed her, then went back into the hole?"

"Yes, I think so," said Babette.

"Well, how come that's not how it happened when we saw it in the mist of Demeter's well? Hades grabbed Persephone, jumped into the chariot, and flew away. The hole closed up, and Hades never went back into it. What he did was fly up into the sky with her. And that's what it says here too. It says, 'After Hades grabbed Persephone, he flew to Eleus.'"

Babette said, "Eel-ee-what-sis?" The constant rocking of Horse as he flew had lulled her nearly to sleep. "I'm sorry, Bridget. I wasn't paying attention."

Bridget read to them from the guide book. "Two brothers were in a meadow near Eleus. That's Eel-EE-uhs. One of them herded sheep and the other tended pigs. The two brothers were minding their own business, tending to the animals, when suddenly the earth split open practically under their feet. A dozen pigs fell right into the gaping hole. The sheep ran in every direction. From the sky, a team of black horses dropped down, pulling a black chariot that contained a stern warrior holding a shrieking girl. The horses, chariot, warrior, girl—all disappeared into the chasm. It closed shut right in front of the brothers. And it all happened near Eleus." She looked up at Babette. "I guess you don't know as much about mythology as you let on."

"There are variations of all the famous mythological stories," explained Babette. "It all depends upon who tells the story. Each version is more or less the same, but some of the details are changed. You see, these stories were written down by poets and storytellers. Not by priests. Each poet had his own special way to tell the story. As a result, not all the details are the same every time. The epic poet Homer wrote the most famous accounts, but there are many others. It isn't really that I was incorrect."

"You'd be better off," said Bridget, "if you'd just admit you were totally wrong."

"Oh, for heaven's sake, Bridget," said Beauregard. "What difference does it make? Don't be so touchy."

"Eleus." Bridget tapped the big cat with her index finger. "Here's my point. Eleus isn't the same place as this Delphi where we're heading. Am I right?"

"Oh, no. They're not the same place. But why does that matter?"

"If Eleus is the place where Hades took Persephone," said Bridget, "then why are we going to Delphi to see this Tiresias guy? Why not just fly straight to Eleus and eliminate the middle man?"

Beauregard looked at Babette, "Well, I guess I don't know what to say, except that, even if the earth did open up at Eleus for Hades, there's no reason to think it will open for us."

"Okay, even if you're right about that, here's another thing. This Tiresias did not reside at Delphi. He was a Theban. From Thebes. It says so right here." Bridget tapped the cover of the guide book.

Beauregard wiggled his whiskers. "Do you know, Babette, she may be right. I remember reading about Tiresias in a play called *Oedipus Rex*. That play's not set in Delphi but in Thebes. Tiresias is a Theban! I believe Bridget's right."

"At least you agree with me about that," Bridget said. "So let's get back on track. Barnaby's right. That old priestess probably has Alzheimer's. She just got confused when she told us to go to Delphi. What I say is, forget about going to Delphi. Head," she thumped their guide on the top of her golden forehead, "tell Horse to change course! We're flying to Thebes, not Delphi."

Although Bridget's desire to change course had no discernible effect on Horse, who continued to fly along the same course he had been following since they'd left Demeter's Island, it did produce another argument. Babette thought it a mistake to ignore the advice of Demeter's high priestess.

"In our world," she said, "it may be true that psychics and fortune tellers are silly and unreliable, but in this world, the mythical world, oracles are taken very seriously, even when they are very old. Oracles are sometimes misunderstood, but they are never wrong. If the High Priestess told us to go to Delphi, that is where we should go. I'm sure of it. Head, you tell Horse to stay on course for Delphi!"

Beauregard said he was not sure what he thought. Head kept her mouth clamped shut.

Barnaby said, "The world's dying. That's all I know. Look down there. Even the ocean's turning brown." And in fact the ocean had turned sluggish and dark, as if Poseidon and all the creatures who lived within it had grown moody and ill. "We haven't got time to waste arguing. We've got to make up our minds. Delphi or Thebes?"

"It won't do any good," Head said glumly. While Head agreed that Tiresias was indeed a Theban and that the high priestess had possibly grown confused and sent them to the wrong place, she said it did not matter. "We can't get Horse to change course. You can yell at him all you want, but my beloved has a one-track mind. Once he starts a flight, that's it. No matter what, he will go where he was told to go in the beginning. Or have you forgotten the storm?"

All of them remembered the storm vividly. No matter how loudly they had shouted at Horse to change course, he had flown them straight into the howling wind.

"When we get back to my master's cave," Head said. "I will suggest Hephaestus correct this little oversight in my darling's brain, but until then we might as well settle down and enjoy the flight. Besides, look there, isn't that Delphi? When we get there, we can get directions to Thebes."

"You mean, you don't know where Thebes is?" demanded Bridget. "What kind of guide are you?"

"I know more or less where it is," Head said. "But we had better ask directions. And if we have any sense, before we do, we will consult the Pythoness."

"The who?" yelled Barnaby.

When Head revealed that the Pythoness was another fortune teller, this too led to an argument. Barnaby did not approve of visiting yet another such person. "Some conwoman named after a snake! She'll probably be just as goofy as the last one."

Bridget thought they might at least take a look at her. "You think she might actually look like a snake? That might be cool to see!"

While they approached Delphi, Babette told the others how the chief priestess of the Temple of Apollo at Delphi obtained her strange name. "When Apollo was still very young, there was a Great Flood."

Bridget looked thoughtful, "You mean like the one mentioned in the Bible, Noah's flood?"

"I don't know if it was the same one, but Great Floods are mentioned in many ancient stories. When the flood receded, the world was covered by a deep slime."

"Yuck!" Bridget made a face.

"The world may have been a mess, but never was it more fertile. The thick bed of luscious slime produced all sorts of new things, some good and some not so good. One of the not so good was the Python. No doubt you have heard of the giant snake that lives in Burma. The Python in this story was a hundred times bigger. It could swallow a human being in one gulp. It was so long it could twist its body three times around Mount Parnassus. As you can well imagine, the Python was a great danger to all the people who lived anywhere near it."

Beauregard interrupted, "Of course, some say the Python did not just crawl out of the slime on his own. They say that the goddess Hera brought the enormous serpent to life and sent it to swallow Leto."

"Leto," explained Babette, "is the mother of Apollo and Artemis."

"Hera, Leto, Artemis, Apollo—as I've said before, mythology's one gigantic, never-ending soap opera," Bridget complained. "I don't think I'm ever going to keep all these gods and goddesses straight." She opened the guidebook again and looked up Leto. "It says here Leto, hmm, how do you like that? No wonder Hera was mad at her."

Babette smiled.

"Go on, Bridget," demanded Barnaby, "don't keep it secret. What'd you find out?"

Bridget explained, "Zeus is the father of Apollo and Artemis, that's all." She looked up at Barnaby. "Don't you get it?"

Barnaby shrugged, "So?"

"So?! Zeus was married to Hera, not Leto!" Bridget laughed. "That's why Hera hated Leto. That's why she sent the giant snake after her."

Babette explained, "You see, Zeus was forever fathering illegitimate children, and his wife Hera was angry about it. She often tried to harm those children and their mothers."

"Wow!" Bridget exclaimed. She had her nose in the book again.

"What is it, Bridget?" Beauregard asked.

"I'm reading the part about Apollo and the Python."

"What happened?" Barnaby asked.

Bridget said, "Although very young, Apollo was an expert at using his bow and arrows. He had never killed an animal much bigger than a deer, but he flew to Parnassus. When he found the Python, Apollo stood on top of a hill and shot arrows into the giant snake until the Python's head resembled a pin cushion. To escape, the monster crawled here to Delphi and tried to hide in a cave. But Apollo tracked it down and shot so many more arrows into its body that at last the Python lay dead."

Babette spoke up, "You see, by killing the Python, Apollo became the first monster slayer. Ever since, when heroes go to kill a monster, they first sacrifice to Apollo. It is said that even Heracles, before he fought the Hydra, honored Apollo with a sacrifice."

"That's interesting," said Barnaby. "He must have done it before we got there. But I want to hear more about this person called the Pythoness."

"Oh, yes. Well, let's see," Babette said, "with the possible exception of Tiresias, the Pythoness is the most respected seer of the mythical world. After the death of the Python, Apollo erected his temple here. To honor his great feat of killing the Python, his chief priestess is always called the Pythoness. When we arrive in Delphi, we will find out what she knows about the whereabouts of Tiresias."

A few minutes later, the winged horse landed within the walls of the city of Delphi. He landed beside a large, rounded, conical stone in a completely deserted street.

"That," said Head, when she saw the stone, "is the Omphalos. We are not far from Apollo's temple. How odd." She sniffed. "Usually, there is a crowd of people here waiting to see the Pythoness. Something must be going on."

"Omphalos," said Barnaby, "is a pretty weird name for a rock. It means your belly button."

Babette laughed. "Yes, *omphalos* means *the navel* or *the center*. The ancient Greeks believed Delphi to be the center of the earth, and this stone marks the center of Delphi." She pointed. "Look!"

Two naked men had just come around a corner and were now running straight toward them. Two more men, just as naked as the first pair, rounded the corner. Then a whole mob of naked men came around the corner, chasing after the first four. Bridget, Barnaby, Babette, and the others had to rush to one side of the street to avoid being run over.

"What in the world?" said Bridget. "What are they, nudists?"

Running just as fast as their legs could carry them, the mob of naked men turned a corner and disappeared.

"The Games must be in progress," Head suggested.

"What games?" said Barnaby. "You mean those guys are athletes?"

"The Pythian Games," Head explained. "They are held once every four years. It's all so silly, but it's the sort of thing Apollo enjoys. He founded the Games after killing the Python. Mortals race chariots, lift heavy weights, and run as fast as they can on their spindly legs. As if anyone of any importance cares how fast a mortal runs. Come along now; the temple is that way. That wall marks the boundary of the sanctuary of Apollo. The temple is inside." Her eyes clicked as she gazed at a high wall made of carefully cut stones. "It appears the gate is open. I suppose the guards who usually stand there are waiting at the finish line of the race. Hurry, please. We must find the Pythoness. Or do you plan to let the world die while you loiter here in the middle of the street?"

Inside the wall was a perfectly splendid temple, a fantastic construction of marble blocks, but they had little time to inspect it. They no more than entered the palace when they heard a loud cry for help, followed by a crash, then another one.

"Come here! Come at once! Hurry! Oh!"

"We'd better go help her," said Beauregard. "Don't you think?"

Bridget said, "Do you think the Pythoness is under attack?"

"I am waiting!" yelled the voice. "I am not happy!"

"We had better find out." Babette led the others through the temple.

They turned a corner and entered a room. A sour-faced woman was standing in the middle of a great scene of wreckage. As they entered, she grasped a vase by its throat and flung it as hard as she could against a wall. Pieces of clay flew in every direction.

"How dare you leave me! How dare you! I will have you all killed. I'll have you flayed alive!"

"Are, are you the Pythoness?" Barnaby asked.

The young woman looked up and saw them in the doorway. Her sour expression turned even more so. "So there you are. I will have my lunch now. And then my back rub. Where have you been? I've been crying for help for minutes. Of course, you will have to clean up this mess." She waved at the wreckage all around her. "How dare you keep me waiting?"

"But we're not servants," said Babette. "We've come to see the Pythoness."

For the first time, the young woman looked at them closely. "Who are you? If you are not my servants, how dare you trespass here?"

Head said, "This is not the Pythoness. I have met the Pythoness, and she is a perfectly respectable woman with white hair. This is not her. Certainly not. Tell us where the Pythoness is, young lady. Do not keep us waiting."

The sour-faced young woman frowned. "I suppose you mean my predecessor, the Old Hag. She is dead. I am the new Pythoness, and I am ready for my lunch. Where is it?"

"You are the Pythoness?" gasped Babette.

"I desire milk, sweet milk, and cheese. Hurry up. Go about your business. Do you want me to starve? And bring me some fresh green olives too!"

"But we are not your servants." Babette looked helplessly at the others.

"How tiresome of you. I am very hungry, especially for olives." The woman sighed, kicked some broken crockery out of the way, and plopped herself down upon a low divan. To no one in particular, she murmured, "All of them deserve to be boiled in oil."

"We've come for a consultation," said Head. "If you are the Pythoness, which I doubt." She snapped her lips together to indicate her skepticism.

"How much will you pay?" asked the sour-faced woman. "I do not work cheap, you know."

"Pay?" said Bridget. "We have to pay?" She looked at Babette. "But we don't have any money."

Babette said, "Although we have nothing with which to pay you, we are sure, when you learn the importance of our quest, you will be eager to assist us."

"Don't be absurd." The Pythoness made a dismissive gesture. "If you can't pay, go."

Speaking all at once, Barnaby and Babette told the Pythoness about their desperate mission to save Persephone and prevent the world from starving.

"Don't you know what's happened?" asked Bridget. "The goddess Demeter has cursed the world. Nothing can grow. Everything's begun to die!"

"I see you are drunks," declared the Pythoness. "Obviously, you are followers of Dionysius," She said the name with distaste: Dy-uh-NYE-suhs. "Guards! Throw these beggars out!" As Babette told the others later, Delphi was sacred not only to the god Apollo but also to the god Dionysius, the god associated with wine. Apparently, the high priestess of Apollo's temple had a low opinion of the followers of the rival god.

Barnaby stepped forward. "There's no one else here. Your servants and guards are gone. Really. And you must quit acting like a spoiled child. The world is in danger, and we need your help. We are looking for a famous seer named Tiresias."

No more did Barnaby pronounce the name Tiresias than the Pythoness jumped to her feet. Her face turned red. She advanced upon Barnaby with her fists clenched. "How dare you say that name in my presence? How dare you sully the air of my temple with that horrid man's name?"

In the distance, they heard loud cheers. Apparently, the foot race was over, and someone had won.

"She's jealous," Head snapped. "Look at her. She's envious of Tiresias. It's plain as the nose on her face." Since the Pythoness's nose was large, lumpy, and very red, this remark made her cry out in rage. "Tiresias is the best seer in the world," Head added. "This person is an obvious fraud. I doubt she's ever met Tiresias."

"Ha!" cried the Pythoness. She smiled grimly. "I've never met him, have I? Ha! So I'm a fraud?" She folded her arms and grinned triumphantly at all of them. "Well, if you are all so smart, and I am such an obvious fraud, then why do I know that your precious Tiresias"—she threw back her head and yelped with laughter—"is dead!"

"Dead?" exclaimed Bridget. "How can he be dead?"

"He died of fever months ago. The old coot. He should have died years ago. You have no idea how much business he took from me." Seeing their expressions, she softened her tone. "You may not like me, but I must take care of this temple. Do you have any idea how much it costs to maintain a temple of this size? Obviously not. This is not Thebes. It is Delphi. And here we have standards. We who worship Apollo care about the beautiful. And beauty—take my word for it—is expensive."

"Tiresias is truly dead?" whispered Babette. "But then, what are we to do?"

Beauregard explained to the Pythoness how they had visited Demeter's Island, how the High Priestess had gazed into the mirror brought up from the Well of Demeter, and told them to come here to seek advice from Tiresias.

The Pythoness ignored Beauregard and walked over to Bridget. "Could I see this, please?" She took Head out of Bridget's arms and inspected her carefully. "Real gold?" she asked.

"Of course, I am made of real gold. I am the property of Hephaestus the god. Keep your fingers to yourself, or I shall bite them!" Head snapped at the Pythoness's fingers.

"Hmm." The Pythoness turned to the others and smiled. "Perhaps we can make a bargain after all." She set Head down on one of her tables, picked up a piece of cloth, and draped it over Head, like people place covers over bird cages. "Is there no way to stop its chattering? No? Well, it doesn't matter. I can always melt her into ingots."

From beneath the cloth, Head let out a screech of protest.

"Come with me," ordered the Pythoness. She smiled sweetly. "Although the old man is dead, I know a way for you to meet him. Of course, such a service does not come cheap. In return, you will let me have your funny head. So amusing, a mechanical head that talks—and made of gold too!"

"Make her promise not to melt me!" Head cried. "Make her promise!"

They did make the Pythoness promise to take good care of Head before agreeing to give her up. And Babette added, "You see, she doesn't really belong to us. As she said, Head is the property of Hephaestus. If the god demands her return, you will have to give her up."

"Let me worry about that," said the Pythoness, smiling slyly.

That night, the city of Delphi was full of lights. The celebration of the victor of the Pythian Games was already in progress. Their hostess was eager to be on her way. As Pythoness, she had to preside over the grandest of the celebrations. "Deeper, much deeper!" she ordered. "That's not deep enough yet!" She had gotten Barnaby to begin digging a trench.

Barnaby sighed. The shovel had already caused a blister to form on the heel of his right hand. This plan of the Pythoness to bring Tiresias to them better work after all this, he thought.

As Barnaby dug, the Pythoness complained. According to her, the life of an oracle was no picnic. "You have no idea what it is like to be the mouthpiece of a god. It's exhausting! Each time, after the oracle speaks through me, I have to lay down flat for a full hour. Does anyone think that is easy? And then people complain. Is it my fault if they do not understand the oracle? I merely deliver it. I do not translate it. Let them complain to the god if they grow confused. And if it's bad news!" The Pythoness spit. "They are furious! As if it's my fault. If their ships are going to sink, they are going to sink. The Fates rule us all. Oh, people love to hear good news, but bad news! Bah!"

"Isn't this deep enough?" Barnaby asked hopefully.

In the darkness, it was hard to see, so all of them stepped forward to inspect Barnaby's trench.

"Oh, I suppose," said the Pythoness. "It will have to do. Now, you must pour in the contents of that jug. Then wait."

"Won't you wait with us, Pythoness?" asked Babette. In the moonlight, the Pythoness looked like a kind of ghost. She had wrapped herself in a veil. Of her face, only her large dark eyes were visible. They glittered in the dim light.

"I haven't time to wait. Here are two swords." The Pythoness handed a sword to Barnaby and another to Babette. "Fill that trench to the brim. When the shades come to drink, tell them they must fetch Tiresias, or else they don't get a drop. Not a drop! Wave your swords at them. They are sneaky, so don't nod off. If you doze, they'll drink it dry, and you'll never see your precious Tiresias." She turned on her heel and quickly walked away without saying good-bye.

"But how will we know for sure which one's Tiresias?" yelled Bridget.

Without turning around, the Pythoness yelled back. "He's old, he's blind, and he smells!" She disappeared into the darkness.

Babette, Bridget, Barnaby, and Beauregard were outside the walls of the city, standing on the bank of a river that gleamed in the moonlight. The golden horse, his wings folded, stood not far away.

"I can't hear any insects," said Barnaby. "You know how normally we'd hear insects, locusts?"

"Demeter's curse," said Babette, "has silenced them."

"Barnaby, come on," Bridget said. "Help me with the jug."

As Beauregard and Babette looked on, Barnaby and Bridget got hold of the jug, dragged it to the lip of the trench Barnaby had dug, and tipped it until its contents poured into the hole.

"Ugh! It's blood!" screamed Bridget. "She didn't mention that part." But she quickly regained her composure after Barnaby, tired and dirty from digging the trench, shot her a warning look. "Just pour!" he said grimly.

When they were finished, they stood in a circle around the trench, not sure what to do next.

"How long before they come, you think?" Bridget whispered. "I wish we had more swords. You guys see anything?"

"Not yet," Barnaby whispered grimly.

Babette clenched her sword tightly and jabbed it into the darkness. "Just practicing," she murmured.

Not until half an hour later did the first of them appear. It stood in the shadow of a nearby tree. By then, the smell of blood had drifted in all directions.

"Barnaby?" whispered Bridget. "Babette? You see that? Or am I going nuts?"

Barnaby and Babette pointed their swords at the thing that stood in the darkness.

"You go away!" yelled Barnaby.

"We want to talk to Tiresias," Babette said. She was careful to keep her voice low. "No one can drink, not until Tiresias comes. Do you understand?"

"Yeah, go get Tiresias!" Barnaby jabbed his sword at the thing in the shadow. "Then you can drink all you want!"

"Scram! Shoo!" Bridget waved her fists in the air and made the scariest face she knew. "Go get Tiresias!"

Half a dozen more shadowy things approached their trench in the next hour. Some seemed to be women, some men. They were nearly transparent but one could see their eyes gleaming dully in the moonlight. Each time one of them appeared, Barnaby and Babette waved their swords. Beauregard and Bridget waved their arms wildly. The kids yelled that no one would get to drink a drop of blood until Tiresias came.

The shadowy things were what the Greeks called shades, spirits of the dead; they were all that was left of mortal men and women who had died. As Beauregard explained, the scent of blood drew them to the trench. Somehow, the dead ones escaped Hades' underworld and came to the surface of the earth in hopes of getting a few drops of blood into their insubstantial bodies. The blood would allow them to feel as if they were alive again, if only for a few moments.

Just before dawn, another shade appeared in the shadow of the tree that stood not far from their trench. Although Barnaby shouted and waved his sword, it did not disappear.

"We seek Tiresias," said Babette. "No one may drink until Tiresias comes to us. Go fetch Tiresias, then you may drink your fill."

"You have found him," said the shade. It drifted a few feet closer to them.

"Wait!" yelled Barnaby. The moonlight revealed the shade to be an old man, but Barnaby feared the shade might be an impostor. "How do we know you are truly Tiresias the Seer?"

"Look at my eyes," said the shade. "They are but the ghosts of my eyes, yet can you not see they are blind?" The shade drew closer to them and revealed that his eyeballs were milky white. It gave Bridget a funny feeling to see the damaged eyes, and she shuddered all over.

"If you are truly Tiresias," said Babette, "you will recall how you came to be a seer. Tell us your story, old one. Then you may drink."

"The entire world knows my story," said the shade.

"But we want to hear it from your own lips." Babette glanced back at the others and whispered to them, "It is said that the dead can no longer tell a lie. But I want to hear him tell the story just to be sure."

"Do you recall the story of Actaeon," asked the shade, "the young hunter who saw the goddess Artemis bathing, and so was turned into a stag and destroyed by his own hounds? My story is similar. One day, through no fault of my own, I came upon the goddess Athena bathing. I had no idea who she was and meant no disrespect. Still, the goddess placed her hands upon my eyes and rendered me blind." The shade frowned, as if he was remembering the incident. "Yet, the goddess Athena is merciful. When she learned she had blinded an innocent man, although she did not possess the power to heal my eyes, she gave me inner sight, the second sight that soothsayers have. Ever since, I have seen into the future."

"He really is Tiresias," whispered Babette. She called out to him, "Come. You may drink."

Quickly, the shade drifted to the trench, bent over it, and drank. As dogs drink the water from puddles, he lapped up the blood. When he rose, the kids were surprised to realize Tiresias was more vivid; the blood had entered him and made him more visible. He almost looked like a living man. They could see his pale skin, his wrinkles, his white beard and eyebrows.

"Why have you disturbed the rest of Tiresias?" he asked.

"A terrible thing has happened in the world," explained Babette. "Your master, Hades, the king of all the dead, has kidnapped Persephone, the daughter of Demeter. As a result, Demeter has cursed the world. Already, the plants are dying. The insects have fallen silent. Soon, all living beings will starve. Please, help us, Tiresias. Won't you show us the way into Hades' kingdom?"

"You are mortals," said Tiresias. His toothless mouth moved into something resembling a smile. "If you desire to see Hades' kingdom, you need only wait. Sooner or later, Death will show you the way."

A cold shudder passed over the kids when they understood the shade meant that sooner or later, they would die.

"We must find a way to enter the underworld right away," Barnaby explained. "We have sworn to help the girl Persephone. Please help us, Tiresias."

The shade seemed to contemplate them, not with his blind eyes but with his mind. "Heracles," he whispered at last.

"What?" said Bridget. "Did he say Heracles?"

"Seek out the warrior who helped you when you first came here to our world."

"But why can't you help us yourself?"

"Because I now belong to Hades, I am not permitted to show you how to enter the Dark Lord's kingdom. All I may do is tell you that, of all who are mortal, only mighty Heracles can help you."

Babette and Barnaby tried to find out more from the shade, but Tiresias slowly began to vanish. "Go to the stables of Augeas," he murmured, then disappeared completely.

As soon as he did, other shades appeared, the ones who had brought Tiresias. They clustered around the trench like flies around a soda can.

"Au-JEE-us?" Barnaby pronounced the new name impatiently. "But how in the world are we going to find Heracles again?" he wailed.

Bridget grinned and pulled the guide book out of her pocket. She tapped its cover. "Chill out, you guys. I think I've got an idea so good you're not gonna believe it!"

Chapter 12
The Augean Stables

One summer vacation, Barnaby and his parents drove across the panhandle of Oklahoma. Enormous cattle lots lined both sides of the highway. The cattle crowded together behind fences, as far as the eye could see. It had amazed them that so many cows could be gathered together in one place. Now, riding on Horse, flying over the sprawling cattle yards of Augeas, Barnaby felt he was back in Oklahoma. Cattle dotted the landscape as thickly as ants crawling on a watermelon rind. Cows mooed, dozed, snapped at one another. Their tails twitched. Tens of thousands of cattle were down there.

A pair of sluggish brown rivers bounded the huge ranch of Augeas. "Those rivers don't look too healthy," said Bridget. "You think they're polluted?"

The hooves of the cattle had turned whole areas of the ranch to dirt and dust. Manure was piled deep in the valleys. The dung in the stockyards was piled so high, the mounds seemed ready to grow into small mountain ranges.

When Horse flew closer to the ranch, Bridget, Babette, and Barnaby noticed that the grass in the pastures had all turned brown. The cattle munched mournfully on the dry stalks of hay and barley as if wishing that somewhere they could locate even a single blade of living grass. But here on the ranch of Augeas, as everywhere else in the world, no plant remained alive. Nothing would ever grow again until Demeter lifted her curse, and that could not happen until Persephone was returned to her, safe and sound.

In the guide book, Bridget found some information about Augeas. "It says here his herds were blessed. All his cows were immune to disease. Plus, they were amazingly fertile." She looked down at all the animals. "That must be why there are so many. The book says, of all the people in the mythic world, Augeas was the richest in herds of cattle."

"I can believe it," said Barnaby. "There must be a hundred thousand cows down there!"

"Over there!" cried Babette. She pointed down to a hill side. "Someone's down there. See him?"

The golden horse must also have seen the man because it gracefully landed on the hillside and allowed the kids to dismount.

No sooner did they jump down and stretch than the wind changed. "Oh, man! What stinks?" Bridget pinched her nose. The stench from the stable yards was so putrid, it made tears come to her eyes. The stench made Barnaby sneeze, and Babette turned pale. It made Beauregard stagger and lash his tail.

While they were coughing, sneezing, and wiping away tears, the man on the hillside rolled over to look at them. He was fat. He was perfectly enormous. And filthy. And hairy. He was so red in the face that he re-sembled a rasp-berry ready to burst. His small round eyes were nearly hidden beneath the mounds of his cheeks. His nose was a small thing but very red. The stench had no apparent effect on him. In fact, when he saw his visitors pinching their noses and choking, the fat man began to laugh. "Can't take it! Can't take it! Yuh sissies!" he wheezed.

The fat man reclined upon a couch the size of a king-size bed. Half a dozen servants must have carried it out here to the hillside above the cattle yards for his benefit. Apparently, the fat man liked to look down and see all the animals. On a low table beside the couch was a large platter stacked high with beef steaks. The fat man tossed away the remains of one of these, then wiped his greasy fingers on his cloak.

"Are you Augeas?" asked Beauregard. "Glad to make your acquaintance, sir. Hope we aren't trespassing. We've come a long distance, looking for Heracles. Have you seen him by any chance?"

"I'm Augeas, that's for sure. But who in blazes are you folks?" Augeas looked at them suspiciously. "Are you poor people? I dislike poor people. Don't care for them! They steal, you know. Whoa! What's that?" He sat up slightly to stare at Horse. "Rode in on that, did you? Ahem." He smiled greedily. "Solid gold, ain't it? Guess you ain't poor then." Augeas waved his hand at the vast herds of cattle in the valley below. "I gotta be on the watch for thieves and rustlers. You got no idea." He belched. "Who'd you say you was lookin' for?"

"We are looking for Heracles," Babette told him. " It's very important that we talk to him."

"Yeah," Bridget stepped forward. "You seen him? Heracles, strongest man in the world? Big guy? Huge muscles?"

"Heracles, you say? Have I seen him? Haw!" Augeas's already red face turned such a deep shade of purple that Bridget was scared he was going to have a massive stroke right there in front of her. Augeas wheezed, laughed, choked.

"Have I seen him? I practically own him!"

"Own Heracles?" asked Beauregard. "That can't be. Are you sure we are talking about the same person?"

"Practically own his nephew Iolaus too. Will own 'em both by sunset!"

"Iolaus!" gasped Bridget.

It took Augeas half a dozen minutes to get control of himself. Then, wiping away tears of laughter, he explained that Heracles and his nephew Iolaus had appeared on his ranch the previous day exactly at sunset.

"They come in my house. I give 'em each a glass of wine. Then Heracles has the nerve to make me a wager."

"What sort of wager?" asked Bridget.

"The sort he's gonna lose!" Augeas roared with laughter, the effort of which so exhausted him that he had to lay still for a minute, then mop the sweat off his red face. He sat up slightly, cocking his head. "Hey, you can hear him. Hear that?"

They heard nothing at first, then heard the sound of a blow, then several more.

"What is it?" asked Barnaby. "It's coming from over there." He pointed to a woods at one side of Augeas's ranch.

"He's chopping down trees, that's what. Hey, you know something?" Augeas lowered his voice and beckoned them to come closer. "He's gone mad." He nodded knowingly.

"Maybe you never heard that about Heracles," Augeas declared. "He goes mad from time to time. On account of them snakes. You know what I mean? Them serpents that Hera sent after him when he was a baby."

They did know the story of Heracles and the snakes. While they were flying to Augeas's ranch, Bridget had read it to them from the section of the guidebook devoted to Heracles. When the goddess Hera had learned that her husband Zeus had once more produced an illegitimate son, she had sent a pair of poisonous snakes into Heracles's nursery while he slept in his cradle beside his twin brother. Half an hour later, Heracles's mother, the beautiful Alcmene, awoke to hear one of her babies screaming in terror. Fearing the worst, Alcmene leapt out of bed and ran to the nursery. When she arrived, she found the weaker twin screaming and crying, while his lusty brother Heracles swung the two dead snakes in his chubby fists, playing with them as if they were toys. Heracles had strangled the poisonous snakes the moment they'd entered his bed. That had been his first feat of strength, and it had occurred when Heracles was hardly a week old.

"What a lot of folks don't know," explained Augeas, "is one of them snakes managed to bite him before it died. The venom never killed Heracles. Didn't seem to trouble him one bit. Not at first. But later, from time to time, that poison in his blood makes Heracles go mad." Augeas smiled with satisfaction. "That's what happened to him yesterday when he came to make that wager with me. It don't matter though. A wager is still a wager." Augeas rubbed his hands together greedily. "Once the sun sets, Heracles and his boy Iolaus will be my slaves!"

"But we don't understand, sir," said Barnaby. "What exactly is the wager?"

"I think I know what it is," said Babette. "You know what the condition of this ranch is. When we flew in, we saw the piles of dung. The valleys are full of it. The stockyards, look!"

The mountain-sized piles of dung steamed in the sunlight.

"I ain't cleaned this place in thirty years!" Augeas chuckled, as if rather proud of this dubious achievement. "That was the wager all right. Heracles bet me that he and his boy can clean up my stockyards, my valleys, my stables, all of it, clean up my entire ranch within one day. That means by sundown today. If he fails, then Heracles is my slave for the rest of his life. That's the wager. Plus, his boy Iolaus too. Though him I don't care about. I got a hundred men here just as strong as Iolaus. It's Heracles I want. And it's Heracles I'll soon own!" Augeas flopped back on his couch and roared with laughter.

Gazing at the dung-filled valleys, the two polluted rivers, the filthy stockyards and stables, Barnaby said, "I can't see that Heracles has made much progress, or any, for that matter."

The others remembered the gagging reek that had brought tears to their eyes when they'd first landed on this hill side. The task of cleaning up Augeas's ranch was obviously impossible. Tons of dung were down there, thousands of tons. Could Heracles truly have gone mad? He must have. Who except a crazy man would even think of making such an impossible wager?

"Last night," explained Augeas, "after dark, when he figured I was asleep, Heracles and his boy tore holes in my stable walls. There, see 'em? When I heard about his foolishness, that's when I knew he was mad."

A stone wall ran around the stables and stockyards. Now that Augeas called their attention to it, the kids could see two large breaches in the walls where Heracles and Iolaus had pulled out the stones.

"Heracles carried them stones on his back down to my rivers and flung them in. He's strong, that's for sure. Some of them stones is the size of a full-grown ox. But how's that gonna help? If that weren't the action of a crazy man, what was it?"

"Tossed them in, did he?" said Beauregard. He and Babette exchanged a thoughtful look. Bridget had her nose back in the guide book.

"Since then," Augeas continued, "he's been in the woods, chopping down trees. He's got his boy Iolaus herding the cattle out of the valleys and up to the hilltops. See him, over there?"

Squinting, Barnaby could barely make out Iolaus, the boy who had guided them nearly to Aphrodite's palace. Iolaus was waving his arms and yelling at the cattle, obediently trudging up hill before him.

"Heracles ain't carted away a single basket of dung, not a one," Augeas said happily. "And sunset's only two hours off. He ain't got a chance, not this late in the day."

Babette lifted an eyebrow. "Sir?"

"Yeah?"

"It appears to me Heracles has carried logs to the rivers and built something with them."

"What do yuh mean, built what?"

"Ha!" Bridget looked up from the guidebook. "I should have read this earlier. He's not as crazy as you think." She closed up the book with a bang.

"What do you know? You don't know a thing!" The fat man managed to prop himself up on his elbows. "Who are you folks anyway? You look like foreigners. And I don't like foreigners. Don't trust 'em! You get off of my property!"

"Don't worry, we'll go," said Beauregard. "Sorry to have disturbed you, sir."

"Hey, Augeas," yelled Bridget as she waited for the others to climb back onto Horse. "What was your side of the wager? If Heracles cleans up your ranch, what do you owe him?"

"If it's any of your business, I'd owe him one tenth of my herds. But Heracles ain't gonna win so much as one cow. Not even one calf. Come sunset, he and that boy are my property!" Augeas made this prediction in a loud voice, but suspicion appeared in his small eyes. "What did she mean, built something?" he muttered to himself. He waved his arms, "Slaves! You, slaves! Come here and help me!"

From the house, half a dozen muscular slaves came running.

When Beauregard, Babette, Bridget, and Barnaby were aboard, Horse spread his wings, cantered a few steps, then leapt into the air.

Soon, they were high above the ranch. Horse fully extended his wings and glided on top of an air current.

From the air, Heracles's strategy was obvious. He had carried the huge stones from the two walls to the rivers and thrown them down into the onrushing water to make solid foundations. Then, while Iolaus drove the cattle to high ground, Heracles cut down trees and carried them on his back to the rivers. He used the logs to build dams. Already, two large lakes were forming behind the dams.

By now, Augeas had guessed what was happening. His servants picked up his couch. Lurching and swaying, they carried him down the steep hillside.

"Augeas is trying to get to his stockyard before that water does," said Barnaby. He shook his head in admiration. "I had no idea Heracles was such a first-rate engineer."

"I read in the guidebook," Bridget said, "that Heracles was honored for draining swamps. He's a lot more than just another muscle-head."

The two lakes created by the dams grew even larger. Soon, the two lakes merged into one huge lake.

"Augeas better watch out," said Barnaby. With his finger, he showed the others how the new lake would soon sweep over a small ridge. "See the path the water will take? Down that slope and straight to the stockyard and the stables."

"That's why Heracles knocked holes in two walls!" Babette exclaimed. "That's the part I didn't understand. But now I see."

"See what?" demanded Bridget. "I don't get it."

"Look at Augeas and his men!" Beauregard yelled.

Augeas had reached the first of the walls. His men set him down and were scrambling around the broken wall, trying to plug its gaping hole.

With difficulty, Augeas pulled himself to his feet. He waved his arms and bellowed orders.

"There's no way they can plug that hole," said Barnaby. "Heracles has carried off all the stones."

"I can't believe it," Bridget said, "he's got them shoveling."

Augeas's men were trying to throw dung into the breaches Heracles had created in the walls. From the sky, it was obvious this technique would never work. The holes were too big.

"Look!" yelled Beauregard.

The lake created by the dammed rivers finally rose high enough to top the small ridge. Water began to trickle over the side. It took the course Barnaby had shown them.

"Watch out!" Bridget yelled.

Under the weight of the water, the ridge crumbled, then gave way all at once. A tidal wave of water poured through the hole. With the force of water bursting out of a fire hose, the newly created river leapt down the hill straight for the stockyard.

"I almost feel sorry for them," murmured Babette.

Augeas staggered through the hole in his stockyard wall. He slipped and fell face-first into dung. His men were already covered from head to toe in dung. Three of them tried to pull their obese master to his feet, but they slipped and fell back into the dung.

The water tore through the gap in the first wall, surged into the stockyard. It swirled around Augeas and his men, engulfed them, nearly drowned them. Augeas popped to the surface, disappeared again beneath the water. The surging waves rolled him around and around like a top.

The entire stockyard and the stables it contained became one big swirling lake. Then the water poured through the hole Heracles had created in the second wall. At last, Bridget understood the importance of that second hole; it allowed the water to pour out into the dung-filled meadows and valleys on the other side of the stockyard.

As the water in the stockyard receded, Augeas was left in a puddle. He flopped back and forth like a beached whale.

His men lay gasping not far away from him. Not so much as an ounce of dung remained in the stockyard. The surging waters had washed it clean.

In one half hour, the water cleaned Augeas's entire ranch of its thirty years of accumulated dung. The stockyard, the stables, the valleys, all were washed clean by the swirling waters.

"Wow," murmured Bridget, when it was all over. "You know what it's like?" She grinned at the others. "It's like Heracles figured out a way to flush a giant toilet!"

Horse flew them to the ridge where the mighty Heracles stood beside his nephew, Iolaus. The handsome, strong man looked so splendid standing there in all the glory of his triumph that the kids broke out into cheers.

Heracles grinned at them, then gave Iolaus orders to take charge of the one tenth of Augeas's massive cattle herd that now belonged to him. Perhaps relieved that he did not have to greet the kids, since he had failed to guide them all the way to Aphrodite's temple, Iolaus ran off to do as he was told.

"I haven't forgotten how you helped me defeat the Hydra," Heracles said. "Have you succeeded in your quest? Did you save the girl?"

The kids told Heracles the story of their adventures since they had left him in the Swamps of Lerna.

"We finally got to Demeter's Island," Babette explained, "but we were too late. By the time we arrived, Hades had kidnapped Persephone, and Demeter had cursed the world."

Heracles nodded, "So Demeter has forbidden the plants to grow. I had feared that was the case. Despite the rain that fell last night, the grass here is brown and dead."

"Your cattle will die unless we save Persephone," Babette said quietly.

Heracles frowned as if thinking hard. "It is dangerous to interfere with the Olympians." He looked each of them in the face. "Hades is the brother of Zeus. He is powerful, especially in his own kingdom."

They all knew the story of Hades. While they had flown here to Augeas's ranch, Bridget had read the story of Hades from out of the guide book. Long ago, the three brothers, Zeus, Poseidon, and Hades, had drawn lots for the world. Zeus had won the best parts of the world: all the land, the entire sky, and Olympus, the home of the gods. Poseidon had won the water world: the seas, rivers, and lakes. Hades had won only the underworld, that gloomy place where the dead sigh eternally. Hades was nearly as powerful as his two brothers, but his nature was somewhat mysterious. He received the dead in his kingdom but was rarely seen on earth. The poets described him as gloomy and quiet. Perhaps he was bitter. Heracles was right. It would be terribly dangerous to cross Hades.

Bridget told Heracles the plan she'd conceived when they were outside Thebes. She tapped the guidebook. "One of your Labors is to go to the underworld. It says so right here in this book."

Heracles frowned but did not disagree.

"You must capture Cerberus, the Three-Headed Dog that guards the gates of Hades' kingdom."

"Sounds most unpleasant," sniffed Beauregard.

"Yes, I must capture Cerberus," Heracles agreed. "But what has that to do with you?"

"Take us with you!" said Bridget. "If Persephone never eats any food the whole time she is in Hades, then she will be allowed to leave. It's all here in this book. We have to go there and warn her! Please, help us, Heracles."

"Yes," added Babette, "we need your help more than ever."

Heracles looked at them very seriously. "This journey to the Gates of Hell is very dangerous. Are you sure you dare to make so difficult a journey?"

Barnaby, Babette, and Bridget looked at one another. Beauregard lashed his tail.

"We've promised to help Persephone," Barnaby said.

"All of you are sure you want to go to the Land of the Dead?" Heracles' eyes were brilliant and dark. His mouth was a hard, determined line.

"Yes," said Beauregard.

"Yes, sir," Barnaby said, "we mean to keep our promise and end winter forever."

"*Oui, monsieur,*" Babette said.

Bridget yanked hard on her baseball cap. "You kidding? Darn right, we do!"

"Then I will take you to the Gates of Hades," Heracles said. "But there I will leave you. If you enter the underworld, you must go by yourselves. And do not forget, although you may be admitted into the Dark World, you may never again be allowed to leave, not unless Hades gives you his permission. Do you still want to go?"

They all looked at one another one more time to be sure, then in unison yelled, "Yes!"

Chapter 13
The River Styx

They were standing at the edge of the earth, beside an ominous, slow-moving stream.

"Feel like somebody's watching us?" Bridget asked the others. Hoping that, if anyone was, he might figure she was definitely too dangerous to attack, she frowned ferociously.

"I know what you mean," Beauregard twitched his whiskers. "Every time I turn my head, it's as if, just for a moment, I see something."

Bridget nodded. "Shadows. I see them with my peripheral vision. Then, when I turn my eyes to look, they're gone. What about you, Babette? Think we're being watched?"

"They are just shades," Babette said. "Spirits of the dead, like Tiresias. We are standing on the bank of the River Styx. It marks the boundary of this world, the upper world, and the lower world."

The inky black river looked more dangerous than ever.

Bridget pointed. "You mean, right over there, that's Hades, where all the dead people live?" Despite herself, Bridget shivered. On the way here, flying on the back of Hephaestus's golden winged horse, she had read a little about Hades in the guide book. The word *Hades* was the name of the god who ruled the Land of the Dead, but it also meant the underworld itself. "I wish Heracles would hurry up and get here." Bridget wished in the worst way she had some bubble gum. When she got tense, she liked to have some gum, and she was definitely feeling tense. "He said he'd meet us here. So where is he?"

Shortly before they had left Augeas's ranch, Heracles had whispered the directions to Hades into Horse's ear. Heracles had told them, since there wasn't enough room for him on Horse, he would find his own way to the River Styx.

Barnaby said, "I think those shades must be scared of us. That's why they stay out of sight. They're not used to seeing living people."

Bridget asked, "You think they're people who just died? Maybe they're waiting to get across the river, waiting for what's-his-name, that ferryman guy."

Babette looked at Beauregard. "I don't think they are newly dead."

"What do you mean?"

"I believe they are the shades of those who never received proper burial. They are those who have no coins for Charon the Ferryman."

Bridget nodded vigorously. "I read about that in the guide book. It's sort of yucky. When you die, your relatives are supposed to put a coin under your tongue, so you'll have something to give to Charon. Otherwise, he won't take you across the River Styx. It said in the book that Charon is a miser. All he cares about is those coins."

"In many ancient works," Babette explained, "it is said that those mortals who do not receive proper burial are never allowed entry into Hades' kingdom. The Greeks took the burial ceremony very seriously. They believed that if one is not honored by the living, he or she will receive no honor here either. Those who are never buried or do not possess coins must remain on this lonely river bank forever."

They felt a little sad, thinking of the shades doomed to remain on this bank, honored by no one, forgotten by everyone.

"What do you think is over there?" Bridget pointed across the river. They strained to see the other bank, but it was obscured by mist. "I read in the book that Hades is divided up into different regions."

"It is the region called Tartarus," Babette said.

"TAR-tuhr-us?" Barnaby looked a little uneasy as he said the name. "Where the evil-doers reside?"

Babette looked at Barnaby and nodded yes.

"I wish Heracles would hurry up," Bridget said again.

"Babette, you think he'll stay with us over there?" Barnaby pointed across the river. "I'll feel a lot safer with him watching over us. Especially if that really is Tartarus."

"I think so. At least for awhile. Heracles always keeps his promises. He told us he would stay with us until he encountered the Hound of Hell, but after that he must drag Cerberus into this world. He has sworn to do so."

"Maybe we should talk a little more about this," Barnaby said. "I mean this is a pretty big step, entering the underworld."

Beauregard lashed his tail. "We still have time to change our minds. You know what else Heracles told us. Very few living people have ever crossed over the River Styx and entered the underworld. And of those few who did, almost none ever returned."

"I read in here"—Bridget waved the guide book—"that Hades hates to let anyone leave his kingdom. I mean, really hates it."

"Did you ever hear the story of Asclepius?" asked Babette.

"Don't think so," Bridget said.

"Since we haven't anything to do until Heracles comes," Beauregard said, "why don't you tell it, Babette?"

"As-KLEP-ee-us, as his name is pronounced, was the greatest healer of the mythical world. Some say he was the son of

Apollo, who is the god of healing, and that Apollo may have taught him many secret remedies. In any case, Asclepius became so accomplished a healer that at last he learned to cure even the dead."

"Even the dead!" exclaimed Bridget. "Whoa!"

"Asclepius did not restore very many to life, only a few. And some say, for his fee, he demanded a huge price in gold. But despite the fact that Asclepius cured only a few of the dead, Hades was outraged to lose even those few. So far as he was concerned, Asclepius was a thief. No god will allow himself to be robbed by a mortal. Hades went to his brother Zeus and complained. He demanded justice. Hades complained until Zeus killed Asclepius with a thunderbolt." Babette looked at the others. "You see what a risk we take if we cross this river. We may become Hades' property."

"I've always looked after you kids," Beauregard stood on his hind legs and looked each of them in the eye. "But this is the most dangerous thing we've ever tried. As I said, we can still change our minds. How about it? Do we really want to cross this river?"

Behind them, a voice said, "The cat speaks the truth."

They whirled to see who it was.

"Heracles!" Bridget cried happily. And there he was, as huge, strong, and handsome as ever. His lion skin was draped around his shoulders. At his side hung his bow and a quiver of arrows. In his hand was his huge club.

They wanted to know how he'd come here, but Heracles only smiled mysteriously. Apparently, he had his own secret ways of getting around the world.

"The kingdom of Hades is dangerous," Heracles said. "Although I can lead you into the underworld, once there, I must capture Cerberus. After that, I will no longer be able to help you. You shouldn't think that there is any dishonor in changing your mind."

Babette looked down at the ground. Barnaby and Beauregard stared at one another. Bridget bit her lower lip.

"We've promised to help Persephone," Babette reminded them. "And end winter."

"When you made this promise," Heracles said gently, "you did not fully understand the danger."

"I understand it now," said Barnaby, "and I guess I still want to save her." He grinned. "Besides, I really hate winter!"

Bridget lifted her head and grinned. "I was hoping somebody else would feel like that."

Babette smiled crookedly. "And you, Monsieur Beauregard? How do you feel?"

"If Barnaby and Bridget are willing, I say, let's give it a try."

Babette ceased to smile. She looked very serious indeed. "Then it is decided. We will cross the river."

Heracles called out, "It is good you have made a decision. Look, the ferryman comes."

From out of the mist came a boat. A shrouded figure stood up in it.

"You think that's Charon?" Bridget whispered.

The boat came closer and closer. The cloaked figure pushed it toward them with a long wooden pole.

"Here, I have one of these for each of you." Heracles handed each of them a golden coin. "When Charon extends his hand, drop in the coin. But be careful not to touch his hand with your warm fingers, or else he will guess that you are still alive."

"We're supposed to pretend we're dead?" Barnaby asked. "How do we do that?"

Heracles stepped between the approaching boat and the kids. "Do not smile. The dead never smile. Do not forget that Charon is a miser. When he holds your gold in his hand, he will not want to give it up. Besides, it is not Charon's duty to drive away living intruders. That chore belongs to Cerberus."

"I suppose dogs have to be put to some use," said Beauregard haughtily.

"What does Cerberus do to intruders?" Barnaby asked. "Or maybe I shouldn't ask."

Heracles laughed. It was a short, sharp laugh, almost like a bark. "He eats them!"

These Greek heroes are tough, Bridget thought. Heracles reminded her of her favorite major leaguers. When there was trouble, Heracles faced it. He even took a certain grim pleasure in facing danger. Heracles was like a really good hitter facing a twenty-game winner with a 90 m.p.h. fastball. A truly good hitter liked to face a pitcher that great; he loved the challenge. Heracles was the same way. Even when he had to walk straight into Hades and tackle Cerberus, the Hound of Hell, Heracles did not lose his nerve. If he had butterflies in his stomach, you would never know it. Bridget just hoped she would not chicken out either.

The kids stayed close behind Heracles, so that Charon could not get a good look at them.

Charon poled the boat to shore. He was a surprisingly small man, and his boat was old, patched, and weather-beaten. Gravel crunched beneath its hull.

Bridget thought that it was hard to know if Charon was alive or dead, mortal or immortal. He seemed a kind of blank, a being only partly alive. His body was concealed by a black cloak. His head was hidden by a black hood.

Charon said nothing but waited patiently for any who wanted to board his boat. Extending his arm, he held out his hand, palm up, for money. Bridget wondered if Charon was all that was left of a mortal who cared about nothing except money. She thought, he's so low that he even takes money from the dead.

Heracles glared steadily at Charon. With his foot, he held the boat to the bank. "Go on, board," he told the kids.

Although Charon moved uneasily, he continued to say nothing. Did the ferryman guess they were alive?

Babette went first. She dropped her coin into Charon's hand. Bridget, Barnaby, and Beauregard came after her. Each of them dropped a coin into the cold narrow palm. They were careful to do as Heracles had told them. They never smiled; they made sure their warm fingers did not touch the cold hand of the ferryman, and they stared down at their feet as if they were sad.

"Too many!" said the ferryman. When Heracles tried to board the boat, Charon shoved hard with his pole. Any mortal except Heracles would have lost control of the boat and fallen back stranded on the riverbank, but Heracles hardly moved. He kept his foot in the boat, and held it down so hard that the boat never moved an inch no matter how vigorously Charon shoved on his pole.

"You will take one more." Heracles stepped into the boat.

"My gold!" Charon shrieked. It was like a cry of pain. Perhaps no one had ever boarded his boat without handing him a piece of money.

"You will get no coin from me until I return, bringing Cerberus with me," Heracles said.

"Bah!" Charon shoved with his pole. The boat entered the river. Designed to accommodate only Charon and one other passenger, the boat soon settled deep into the river. The black water began to slop over its sides.

"Too many!" cried Charon.

"Push!" Heracles demanded.

"Too many," whispered Charon. His voice was low and mournful as the wind on a stormy night.

"Push," Heracles said, "or I will push for you." Heracles was so stern, so determined that even the kids began to be a little afraid of him.

The boat did not sink as it crossed the river, but an inch of inky black water slopped into the boat. The kids did not want to touch the strange liquid, but it crept into their tennis shoes and turned their toes icy.

With great relief, Barnaby, Babette, and Bridget heard gravel crunch beneath the hull. They had safely crossed the River Styx. One by one, they leapt out of the boat and set foot upon the soil of Tartarus.

"So this is where the evil people go, huh?" Bridget peered into the mist. She almost had the idea she might see the ghost of Hitler drifting around this strange place.

"Stay together," Heracles said. "There are many dangers here." His eyes never stopped moving. They suddenly had the idea that this gloomy place really was dangerous. Cerberus, the Three-Headed Hound of Hell, might leap out of the fog at any moment. They walked in a bunch, right at Heracles' heels. "No matter what else you do while you are here," Heracles said, "never eat anything."

They nodded, recalling the story about Persephone eating the six pomegranate seeds.

"Don't worry," Bridget said. "I'm definitely not eating anything!"

"Do not drink anything, either," Heracles said. "No matter how thirsty you are."

Bridget swallowed. Already, her throat felt dry.

The region called Tartarus was large and dark, dismal and misty, but it did not contain many shades. The ancient Greeks did not believe that many humans were really so wicked as to deserve eternal torment. As they crossed this region, the kids were careful not to fall into any holes. Puddles were everywhere. The region was so damp, so cold and dismal that they all began to get a little depressed. They remembered the old saying, "Better to be the slave of a poor man than to rule in Tartarus."

"Look," Barnaby whispered, "that guy, see him?"

The guy was a skinny, half-naked man standing in a pool of water beneath a tree. On the man's face was an expression of incredible agony and weariness. The water in the pool was clear, not muddy at all. It looked almost delicious. But as they got closer to him, Barnaby, Babette, and Bridget could see the man's lips were parched and cracked as if he had not had a drink in days. He was so thin they could see his ribs. A tree branch hung just over his head.

"I can't believe it," Barnaby whispered. "I thought it was an apple tree but look, there's all different kinds of fruit growing on that same branch." It seemed impossible, but Barnaby was right. The tree branch was loaded with apples, pears, oranges, and figs.

The skinny man gazed hungrily at the fruit; he raised his hand to pick an apple. A sudden gust of wind tossed the branch up out of reach of his fingers.

"Tantalus," Babette whispered. "Can it be?"

Heracles nodded. "Do not go too close to him."

As they hurried around the pond, Heracles told them a little about Tantalus. "Once, this mortal was a friend of Father Zeus himself. No other mortal was so honored. Tantalus was allowed to dine with the gods; he was served nectar and ambrosia, the special food of the gods. But he was an ungrateful thief. To impress his friends on earth, he stole the divine food and took it home."

"Was that his only crime?" Bridget asked. "I mean stealing is pretty bad, I guess, especially when you steal from people who are being nice to you, but—"

"Tantalus did something much more horrible. Because he was the friend of Zeus, he came to believe he was just as great as the gods, and that in fact the gods were not special. To prove that even Zeus could be fooled, Tantalus did an evil thing. He murdered his own son."

The kids gasped. They turned around to look at Tantalus. The tormented man reached down to get a handful of the clear, fresh water. The moment he did, the level of the water sank. The farther down Tantalus bent, the lower the pond sank until it was nothing but mud. When Tantalus stood up straight again, the water rose up around his knees.

"Now I know where the word tantalize comes from," said Barnaby, shaking his head.

"Tantalus cut up his son and made him into a stew. He invited the gods to eat at his house and served them this miserable stew," continued Heracles.

"Wow!" Barnaby said.

"Yuck!" Bridget said. "Did they eat it?"

"Zeus was not fooled. You see how Tantalus is punished. Because he stole from the gods, because he murdered his own son and tried to serve disgusting food to the Olympians, Tantalus must stand forever in that pool. Each time he bends down to drink, the water sinks. When he tries to eat from the fruit tree, the branch is blown up out of his reach. He suffers eternal hunger and endless thirst."

Not too much farther, when they were nearing the border of Tartarus, they heard a loud rumble. Nearby was a steep hill. An enormous stone rolled down the hill, came to a stop at its foot. An old man wearily climbed down the hill. He put his shoulder to the boulder and heaved. Slowly, he rolled the stone up the hill.

"Is it Sisyphus?" asked Babette.

While they watched the old man heaving and straining against the boulder, pushing it ever farther up the hill, Heracles told them a little about Sisyphus. "He was the sort of villain who invites travelers into his home and then kills them for their money. But his worst crime occurred here in the underworld. Sisyphus was so crafty a criminal that he tricked the Lord Hades by showing him a pair of manacles."

"You mean, like handcuffs?" Barnaby asked.

Heracles nodded. "When the god Hades put them on his wrists, he found himself trapped. Sisyphus kept the god a prisoner in Hades' own palace. Because he was a prisoner, Hades ceased to send Death into the upper world. As a result, no one died. You might think the mortal world a better place without Death, but you would be mistaken. The very old and extremely sick could not die. Warriors with hideous mortal wounds could not die either. Even criminals who had been beheaded could not die. Their headless bodies continued to move. All such people prayed for Death to relieve them of their suffering, but Death could not come, not unless given permission by Hades."

With one last incredible shove, the old man pushed the boulder to the top of the hill.

"Finally, the god Ares—"

"Ares is the god of War," whispered Babette.

"—was so offended by the sight of warriors maimed in battle, unable to die, littering his battlefields, that he came down to the underworld and rescued Hades."

The boulder tottered, teetered.

"For his crime against Hades, Sisyphus must push that boulder up the hill."

Despite the frantic efforts of the old man to keep the boulder at the top of the hill, the great stone broke loose, rolled and bounced down the hill. Sisyphus stood at the top of the hill, gazing mournfully down at the stone, then wearily began his descent.

"But as you can see, no more does Sisyphus push the great stone to the hill top than it rolls back down, and he must push it back up again. He must repeat this useless task until the end of time."

"Is there no happy place here?" Barnaby asked. "What happens to people who are not evil?"

Heracles led them to the top of the hill. Behind them was the dark and gloomy region of Tartarus. But on the other side of the hill was a long flatland. It was overcast, gloomy, but not nearly so dismal a land as Tartarus. "That sunless region is known as the Asphodel Meadows," Heracles said. "It is to that place that the great mass of humankind is sent, those who are neither especially good nor truly evil. It is a sad place, full of sighs, but the shades who live there are not punished."

"But what about the really good people?" Bridget asked.

"They live in Elysium," Heracles said, pronouncing it Ill-IZ-ee-um.

Babette nodded. "Some people call it Elysian Fields."

Heracles smiled. "Elysium is a beautiful land where no one is ever unhappy. Day never turns into night. There is no cold or snow."

"Wow," Bridget said, "if we save Persephone and end winter like we plan, maybe the whole world will be like Elysium. You think?"

"It will be as the Fates will," said Heracles. "This way. We must cross the edge of the Asphodel Meadows."

When they finally crossed the Meadows and saw their destination, they stopped dead in their tracks. The Palace of Aphrodite had seemed to float in the air like a cloud; Apollo's palace had been radiant and magnificent, like a castle made out of light, but when they came upon Hades' dark palace, they saw it was unlike any habitation they had ever seen. The Palace of Hades rose up from the earth like a monstrous outcropping of black rock. There were no windows, only a series of steps that led up to a massive set of doors.

"This is worse than Alcatraz," whispered Bridget.

"You must wait for me here," Heracles said. "I will climb up and call for Hades to release Cerberus. If I am unable to see you again, may the gods prevent you from harm." He struck his chest with his bare hand.

They all managed to say good-bye, and none of them cried, but each of the kids felt a little like it. So long as Heracles had been their guide, they had not been afraid.

"Thank you very much, sir," Barnaby said, "for watching over us."

"We really appreciate it, big guy," Bridget said.

"Adieu," said Babette. Beauregard graciously waved his long tail and saluted.

Heracles began to walk up a trail that led to the Palace of Hades. But he did not get very far before a low, rumbling voice spoke out of thin air.

"Does Heracles dare to enter my world without permission? Stop right where you are."

Heracles turned slowly. "Show yourself, Lord Hades." His hand tightened on his club.

The kids looked every which way but could see no one. Yet, the thunderous voice had been unmistakable.

"I have come for Cerberus," Heracles' eyes gazed steadily at the place from which the voice had come, but no one stood there. "Remove your helmet, Hades," Heracles smiled mockingly, "or does the Lord of the Dead fear to be seen?"

"Bah! I fear no one!"

Slowly, a form became visible. At first, the kids could see only a faint shimmer, then they made out the silhouette of a huge warrior. At last, they could see him clearly. A massive god, as tall and muscular as Heracles, stood on the path. He wore black body armor. In his hands, he held a helmet. (Later, Babette explained to the others that the helmet was one of Hades' most prized possessions. It caused its wearer to become invisible. Not until Hades removed it could any mortal see him.)

"I seek no fight with you, Lord of the Dead, but I must ask you to release the Hound. I have sworn to capture him."

"What do I care what you have sworn?" The dark eyes of Hades flashed angrily. "Cerberus will devour you and these little ones too."

The kids huddled together. "Who's he calling a little one?" Bridget muttered.

"Call Cerberus." Heracles eyes flashed. "We will see how sharp his teeth are."

"Why should I allow you to fight my faithful beast?"

"So great is my admiration for you," Heracles said, "that I would have your permission, Lord Hades. Although I fear you not, my respect for you is genuine. Grant me permission to try my strength against that of the Hound."

Hades did not smile, but his mouth became like a thin sharp cut. "Will you fight on my terms?"

"I am your guest, my lord."

"Then, lay down your club and put aside your arrows. It is my pleasure to see you fight my pet bare-handed."

Heracles smiled grimly, but he tossed away his club. He lay down his huge bow and set his arrows beside it.

Hades waved his arm in the air.

"Will you call for the Hound?" Heracles asked.

"Cerberus will come," Hades said. "Look up there."

Barnaby, Bridget, and Babette heard the Hound long before they saw him come through the doors of Hades' Palace. They heard a rumble, a growl—in fact, a mixture of growls—sounds so low and powerful they made the earth shake the way a stereo does when the bass is turned up high as it will go. As for Beauregard, he heard the howling sounds too and responded with a nonchalant shake of his tail, although Barnaby thought he detected a bit more elevation than usual in the big cat's fur.

The beast bounded out of the palace doors. He was huge. No dog on earth was half so large as the Hound of Hell. The body of Cerberus was slender, muscular, but he was the size of an ox. His paws were huge, his claws long as those of a grizzly bear. His legs were long and well-muscled. Cerberus paused at the top of the path to gaze hungrily down at Heracles.

"Come, my pet," the god Hades cried, "this one would try your teeth."

The most horrible aspect of Cerberus was not that it possessed three heads, each of them like that of a mastiff, or that each head had a gaping mouth full of fangs and grinders, but that around each head was a thick mane of serpents. The poisonous snakes writhed, twisted, and hissed. The Hound trotted eagerly down the path. Its trio of heads kept their eyes fixed on Heracles, who stood waiting for Cerberus with his feet planted, his arms outstretched, in a half crouch like that of a wrestler.

There was something dead but intent in the eyes of Cerberus. His eyes were flat, dead, and yellow, more like snake-eyes than the warm eyes of a real canine. Three long brown tongues dangled down from three sets of jaws. Saliva dropped from these tongues and fell hissing onto the ground.

"Be careful, Heracles!" Bridget yelled. "Even his drool is poison!" She had read this disturbing fact about Cerberus in the guide book.

"Absolutely disgusting," said Beauregard, seeming all too indifferent to the fearsome hound who faced Heracles.

Cerberus and Heracles warily circled one another. The Hound had its three mouths open. Its yellow fangs glowed eerily in the wan light of this world.

The eyes of Heracles were bright, almost merry. His face was flushed, but he breathed calmly. The great hero moved nimbly as a dancer, leaping safely away each time the Hound lunged at him. The massive heads snapped the air; the rows of teeth crashed together. The serpents around the three heads never ceased to twist and writhe. Their triangular heads darted at Heracles and tried to sink their fangs into the flesh of his arms.

"Go, dog!" Hades cried. "Take him now!"

Cerberus lunged forward, but Heracles leapt to one side, not so far as before. The moment his feet touched the ground, he changed direction. Heracles was behind Cerberus before the Hound understood what had happened. Heracles leapt up onto the Hound's back. He locked his huge arms around Cerberus's neck, right at its base where the three heads joined the Hound's body. The snakes bit at him, but Heracles' neck and shoulders were protected by his thick lion pelt. Cerberus went into a frenzy. The Hound leapt, spun; finally it rolled onto its back, trying furiously to dislodge Heracles. But the hero would not let go. He hung on like death. No matter how Cerberus flung himself from side to side or rolled on the ground, Heracles tightened his grip until he choked off the Hound's breath. He squeezed until he nearly crushed Cerberus's windpipe. The throttled Hound staggered and fell to its knees.

"Bah!" Hades cried in disgust.

The Hound's eyes bulged until it seemed they would burst out of their sockets. The three tongues turned black. The only sound now was that of the Hound, choking, gagging.

"Submit!" Hades cried. "Or else he will kill you."

The Hound's legs buckled; its chest crashed to the ground. The three massive heads fell to one side; the snakes hung down limp as the strands of a wet mop.

"You've won," Hades said. "I admit defeat."

Not until then did Heracles loosen his grip. He said nothing but half-dragged, half-carried the stupefied Hound back the way he had come, toward Charon's ferryboat.

Not until Heracles and Cerberus were a hundred yards down the path did the kids realize the fight was truly over. Heracles had won the biggest fight of his life!

"Where's he taking Cerberus?" Barnaby asked.

"He's promised to bring the Hound of Hell to a king called Eurysthesus," Babette said. "Dragging Cerberus out of Hades to the upper world is one of the most famous of Heracles' Twelve Labors. Now, the mighty Heracles really is fit to become a god."

The kids watched until the hero and the Hound of Hell disappeared. They felt like cheering. They felt as if they'd just watched the greatest wrestling event in the history of the world.

And then they remembered that they were all alone in the Land of the Dead. And Hades, the Dark Lord of this world, was angry, and he was staring right at them with his cold yellow eyes.

Chapter 14
Hades

Barnaby admired Babette tremendously. Maybe she wasn't as good as he was at science, but who was? Babette had one of the quickest and most devastating karate kicks anyone would ever see. She spoke an amazing number of languages. Babette was a walking encyclopedia on the subject of Greek mythology. How could you help but admire somebody like that? Plus, she was cool. You never knew what Babette was thinking behind those sunglasses. Barnaby figured Babette was one of the coolest people he had ever met in his life. It was a thrill to be her friend. But never had Barnaby seen Babette so cool as she was the day she looked the Lord of the Dead straight in the eye and asked, "Do you love Persephone?"

Still angry that Heracles had dragged off his dog Cerberus, Hades looked at Babette as if he wanted to bite her head off.

Babette did not even step backward. She actually took a step closer to Hades. If she was even slightly nervous, you would never guess it. "Because if you do love Persephone, then why do you make her miserable?"

"Miserable? How dare you say this to me in my own kingdom?"

"Where is she?" Babette demanded. "We will ask her if she's happy. I think you are keeping her a prisoner here. And it's obvious you do not love her at all. If you love someone, you do not keep her a prisoner. You make sure she is happy."

"Happy?" said Hades. "Of course she is happy."

"Ha!" Bridget rushed to Babette's side to defend her. "I bet he doesn't even know what the word *happy* means. He probably thinks it's normal for her to be sighing and crying all the time."

"Persephone is Queen of Hades." Hades' voice was a low thunder.

Maybe Babette was scared, but she did not flinch. "We want to help her. Where is she? Could we speak to your prisoner?"

"Help her? How dare you imply her Majesty requires help from mortals?! Bah!" The god turned on his heel and strode rapidly toward one end of the palace, where a tree grew beside a pool.

"Come." Babette motioned to the others. "We must follow him."

Babette, Barnaby, Bridget, and Beauregard marched behind Hades until they arrived at the pool of water. The tree that hung over it was a white cypress.

As soon as Babette saw the cypress tree, she said, "I know what this place is." She pointed at the dark water. "That is the Pool of Lethe. Anyone who drinks of that water soon forgets all the details of her mortal life. You thought you would find Persephone here, didn't you? She is not here."

Hades frowned. His forehead wrinkled; his eyebrows lowered. He glared at Babette as if he was ready to cast her into a pit of ever-lasting fire.

"I think we both can guess where Persephone is," Babette said.

"Bah!" The god Hades turned on his heel and strode rapidly in the direction he had just come, toward the other end of his massive palace.

The kids ran to keep up with Hades, but it was impossible. Like all the gods, Hades wore magical shoes made by Hephaestus. He could move as quickly as the wind, as swiftly as he desired.

"What's going on, Babette?" Bridget tapped her friend's elbow. "Where's he going? How'd you know that was the Pool of—what'd you call it?"

"Lethe," Babette said, "the Pool of Forgetfulness. In many of the accounts of Hades, we learn that at one end of Hades' Palace, beneath a white cypress tree, is the Pool of Lethe, the Pool of Forgetfulness. Hades truly does love Persephone. That's what I'm counting on. Incredible as it seems, he also believes she loves him. That's why he thought Persephone was here. He thought she wants to forget her former life on the Island, that she wants to forget her childhood and her friends, even her mother."

"But she isn't here," Bridget said.

"So where is she?" asked Barnaby.

"At the other end of Hades' Palace is another pool, the Pool of Memory. It stands beneath a white poplar tree. I believe that is where Hades will find Persephone."

"Wow," Bridget whispered, "the Pool of Memory. You know what, Babette, sometimes you are so smart it's sort of scary!"

"I believe he will find Persephone sitting above it, gazing down into it, and remembering all that she has lost: her mother Demeter, her friends, those lovely, sun-drenched fields where she danced and collected flowers each day."

"Excuse me," said a cheerful voice, "could you direct me to the Lord Hades?"

A very handsome young man smiled at them. He wore a golden hat with a wide round brim, carried a golden stick adorned with white ribbons. Golden wings were attached to the heels of his shoes. A small leather bag was attached to his waist. "I must deliver a message." His eyes grew wide as he looked at them. They were very merry, bright eyes, as merry and bright as the eyes of a mischievous child. "Why, I know who you are! The outsiders!" The young man bowed slightly. "Happy to make your acquaintance."

"The outsiders?" Barnaby asked. Who was this guy? Despite his funny shoes and weird golden hat, it was impossible not to like him.

"The travelers," the young man made a comical face, "from another world, another time! Oh, don't worry. I know all about you. I'm supposed to fetch you straight to Olympus."

"To Olympus!" Bridget said. She'd read about Olympus in the guide book. It was the home of the gods. Who in the world could be sending for them? Who was this cute guy? And how did he know so darn much about them?

"Zeus himself, my master, has issued an invitation. Don't worry! I will carry you there myself." He bowed again. "But first, I must find the Lord Hades. Where is he? Have you seen him?"

Babette extended her hand. The young man at once grasped it, bent over it, and kissed it. "Ah, you must be Babette!"

"And you," Babette said, smiling, "must be Hermes."

"At your service." The young man bowed again. He was really wonderful about bowing, performing each bow with extraordinary grace.

Bridget racked her brain, trying to recall everything she'd read in the guide book about Hermes. He was the messenger of Zeus and could fly about the world as fast as thought. That was why he had those winged shoes. And the round hat was to keep the rain from splashing down his face. The golden rod with the white ribbons was his herald's staff; it showed he was the messenger of Zeus and so should be respected.

"This way," Babette motioned toward the far end of Hades' great, dark palace. "We think Hades is with Persephone, and that both of them are standing at the edge of the Pool of Memory."

Afterward, Bridget, Barnaby, and Babette were not at all sure how it happened. One moment, they were standing not far from the Pool of Lethe, at the right side of Hades' Palace. The next moment, they were standing at the left end of the palace beside the Pool of Memory. It all happened in a twinkling. Somehow, Hermes had transported all of them from one end of the palace to the other.

"My Lord Hades"—Hermes bowed beautifully to the dark god of the underworld—"may I have permission to speak? I bring you an urgent message from your brother, His Majesty Zeus."

Perhaps it was their sudden transport from one end of the palace to the other that made them dizzy. Or perhaps it was the girl. None of them could think. What a lovely girl. She was dark and sad. Pale. There is something about beauty that renders people speechless. And so it was this time. Persephone was the most beautiful goddess they had seen, as beautiful as Aphrodite but in a strange and new way. No wonder Hades loved her. Persephone was delicate and sad. Her eyes were dark and enormous. Her skin was pale as the lily. She was slender, graceful. But there was nothing weak about her. That was what most surprised them. All this time, they had thought of Persephone as a victim: the helpless prisoner of Hades, the Dark God. But she was splendid and proud. Despite her air of sadness, she really did seem a queen. Persephone seemed like the tragic heroine of a fine old play, a young queen, magnificent and sad.

Hades did not turn his eyes from Persephone, but he motioned with a hand, giving Hermes permission to speak.

"Zeus asks that you bring Persephone to Olympus. Her mother, the great goddess Demeter, has been to see him.

Demeter now knows that it was you, my Lord Hades, who took away her daughter. She demands Persephone's return. The goddess has withdrawn her blessing from the world. No plant grows. No flower blooms. No tree bears fruit. All the world will die unless you restore Persephone to Demeter. Zeus asks you to do as he requests as a personal favor to him. In return, he will give you any woman you want, any who lives in the whole world." Hermes bowed again. "What say you, my Lord Hades?"

"I want no other." Hades' voice was low and soft.

"Then come to Olympus. Appear before Zeus and make your case. Let Father Zeus judge this matter."

Throughout this exchange, Hades never once ceased to gaze at Persephone, nor did she cease to gaze at Hades. There was between them some deep and silent communication.

"If all the Olympians stand against me," said Hades, "I will resist them. I will close the gates of my kingdom and declare war upon heaven. I will fight the Olympians, all of them, even my brother Zeus. The oceans may dry up, and fire consume the earth. All the world may die, but I will never give up the one I love. Deliver this message to my brother Zeus. Now, leave my kingdom." Hades turned to glare at Hermes. His huge hands became fists. His eyes flashed black fire.

Hermes did not withdraw. He lifted his head and gazed coolly at the Lord of the Dead.

"My lord," said a soft voice.

Hades' mouth was a grim straight line. His face grew dark as a thunder cloud. He seemed ready to strike Hermes.

"May I speak, my lord?"

As if awakening from a dream, Hades shook himself. He turned from Hermes to look at Persephone, for it was she who had spoken. "My dear, you need not ask my permission to speak." He looked back at Hermes and grimaced angrily.

"My lord, I have your love?" Persephone touched Hades' massive forearm. It was a small, gentle gesture, yet it transformed the dark god. He looked down at her; his eyes softened. "Whatever you desire, even if it is the throne of Zeus himself, I will obtain for you."

"It is my wish that we accept Zeus's invitation."

"Bah!" The god of the underworld frowned bitterly. Then he stood tall, nodded. "It will be as you wish." He turned to Hermes. "Tell my brother he may soon expect to receive us. Now, leave our kingdom."

"All shall be as you desire, my Lord Hades." The god Hermes, every inch the messenger of Zeus, bowed deeply.

Hermes carried them to Olympus in a net that stretched and stretched until it held all of them. Hermes bunched them together, wrapped the net around them, and flung them over his shoulder as if he were Santa Claus and they were the bag of presents. It was definitely not a comfortable flight.

As they flew out of the underworld, Hermes swooped down so they could see the Land of the Dead from above; it was divided by its great rivers, the River Styx and its tributaries. They saw Sisyphus still pushing his stone, and Tantalus still longing for a drink or a bite of fruit. Charon the Ferryman looked up startled when they flew over his head.

Bridget slipped. It was very hard to remain upright in the baglike net that held them. She tilted, then slid some more until she was nearly upside down. Her nose was not far from Hermes' waist. A small leather bag was tied to a thong wound around the handsome young god's waist. It smelled of something. What was it? Some sort of fruit? Bridget slipped again.

"Hey! Watch out!" Barnaby yelled. "Watch what you're doing!"

Hermes flew so rapidly through the air that, inside the net, they tumbled every which way. Barnaby stepped on

Beauregard's paw. Beauregard somehow tickled Bridget's chin with his tail. Bridget elbowed Babette, who stuck her toe in Barnaby's eye. By the time Hermes flew past Thessaly and up the steep slope of Mt. Olympus, all of them were as exhausted and peevish as kids who've been penned up for too long by their vacationing parents in the back of a minivan.

"Are we there yet?" Bridget demanded. "Barnaby, I mean it. If you poke me one more time, I'm gonna clobber you!"

"Oh, shut up, Bridget. I think my leg's gone to sleep."

"Look, look," Babette whispered. "Up there—the mountain's summit."

And then Bridget, Barnaby, and Beauregard saw it, a huge gate made of clouds. The clouds were not the pure white kind that look like fluffy cotton balls, but the kind that seem to have soaked up all the colors of the rainbow: pink, purple, rose, blue, and gold. They were a mountain on top of a mountain. The technicolor gate swung open to admit Hermes. It closed when he passed through.

The kids forgot to complain about their discomfort. They were in awe. Below them was the celestial city, a cluster of palaces more handsome than any that exist on earth, more elaborate than the grand cathedrals of Europe, more graceful and elegant than the Taj Mahal. Hermes flew straight to the most magnificent of them all, the Palace of Zeus.

Hermes flew in an open window of the palace and deposited them, none too gently, upon the floor of a small elegant waiting room that adjoined the great hall of Zeus's palace. "You are to wait here until sent for," Hermes told them sternly. "Remember where you are and cause no offense. Do I have your oaths that you will remain here?"

Babette said, "Yes, Monsieur Hermes, I promise."

Barnaby said, "Yes, sir. Of course."

Beauregard said, "Absolutely. Word of honor. Won't move till given permission. Don't worry."

Hermes turned. His every movement was so quick and graceful that it was a kick to watch him. He closed its door behind him, leaving them alone.

The others turned to Bridget who was attempting to look as innocent as she could.

"This is the Palace of Zeus himself!" said Babette.

Beauregard lashed his tail. "My dear, you wouldn't! Not here. We've given our words."

"You mean, you guys gave your words," Bridget said sweetly. She was looking at an object set on top of a low table.

Barnaby said, "This is no time to mess around, Bridget." He tried to see what Bridget was doing. She was bent over the table, picking something up. Was it a golden bowl?

"I've seen this before," Bridget said. "Hey, I know what this is!"

"Bridget, wait! Don't do it!" yelped Babette.

Bridget put the object, whatever it was, on top of her head, and disappeared.

"Hey!" yelled Barnaby.

"This is not funny, Bridget," Babette said. "Take that off at once!"

"Where is she?" Beauregard said. His nose wiggled as he sniffed the air, trying to catch Bridget's scent.

"She can't have vanished into thin air!" Barnaby exclaimed.

"She can," said Babette, "if what she found on that table was Hades' helmet of invisibility."

Beauregard pounced, but did not find Bridget. "I thought I smelled her, the faint aroma of bubble gum," he murmured in disappointment. "If only she still chewed the stuff."

"Bridget, I mean it," Babette said sternly, "you are not to leave this room. You know what we promised Hermes."

"See you guys!"

Before any of them could do anything about it, as if by magic, the room's door opened and closed.

"Oh, no," Babette groaned, "she's done it."

When Bridget tiptoed into the great hall of Zeus's Palace, the Olympians were already gathered there to hear Zeus judge the dispute between Demeter and Hades.

The sight of the gods and goddesses all in one place thrilled Bridget. They were so incredibly good-looking! It was like watching the Oscars ceremony, with all the movie stars gathered together, except the gods and goddesses were even more glamorous than movie stars.

The great hall of Zeus's palace was a huge space surrounded by tall white pillars. It was dominated at one end by a pair of enormous golden thrones. Both of them were occupied.

Trying to be quiet as a mouse, Bridget tiptoed closer to the gods. Wearing the helmet that Hades had left in the anteroom, she was invisible. But if she was not careful, she could still betray her presence by making a noise. Bridget tried not to think about what might happen if the Olympians caught her, a mere mortal, snooping on them. But really, she wasn't going to come this far and miss something so exciting. The occupant of one of the thrones was speaking, but Bridget couldn't quite make out what he was saying. She crept a little closer.

That big, bearded guy on the golden throne, she decided, must be Zeus, the chief of all the gods. And that goddess beside him must be Hera, his wife. Hera was beautiful, of course, splendid from head to toe, but not skinny. Hera was nothing at all like one of those models you see in the fashion magazines. She was strong and robust, a true queen. According to the guide book that Bridget had read, Hera was usually mad at Zeus on account of his numerous love affairs. You couldn't tell it today though. The goddess was listening intently to the proceedings.

The goddess standing in front of Zeus and Hera, facing them, must be Demeter the Great Goddess. Bridget tiptoed around the side of the great hall to get a better look at her. The Great Goddess's eyes flashed with anger, then she turned, looked down at the girl beside her. It was Persephone all right. Demeter smiled kindly when she gazed at her daughter, but the moment she looked up and saw Hades, who was standing on the other side of Persephone, the Great Goddess grew red with anger.

Standing between the powerful goddess and the equally powerful Lord of the Dead, Persephone was touchingly beautiful, but she seemed a little lost. The pale young goddess had bowed her head; she looked down at the floor as if wishing she was far away.

Hades looked proud and angry, as if even the slightest insult to his honor would cause him to declare war upon everyone in the room. Bridget wondered, with a secret thrill, if maybe Hades would scoop up Persephone in his enormous arms and fly off with her, defying Zeus, Hera, Demeter, everyone. That was the power of love, all right. Not even Hades could resist it.

There was Aphrodite, breathtakingly beautiful, as always. Beside her, the young-looking Eros leaned against a pillar and looked bored. Really, when you thought about it, this whole mess was their fault.

Three Olympians that Bridget had never seen before stood to one side. One of them was a powerful god with a long beard. Was that a strand of seaweed dangling from his beard? The god held a three-pronged spear in his right hand. The seaweed and trident made it easy for Bridget to guess he was Poseidon. The god of the Sea listened intently as Zeus spoke.

The tall, regal goddess beside Poseidon must be Athena, said to be the wisest of the gods. She looked on coolly and dispassionately.

Not far from Poseidon and Athena stood Phoebus Apollo and Artemis. Despite the fact that he had been promised Persephone, the sun god did not seem especially concerned with Persephone's fate. Artemis was obviously bored and looked eager to return to her beloved woods.

Not far from where Bridget stood, leaning against a wall, was a huge, bearded god. His eyes glowed red as burning coals. From head to toe he was covered in gleaming armor. Bridget shuddered, guessing he must be Ares, the god of War. According to the guide book, never did that god experience joy except when men fought and blood flowed.

Bridget still could not hear very well. She crept closer to the gods and goddesses. Oh, it was impossibly romantic. It was like watching the climax of a good movie, except a thousand times better because you could almost reach out and touch all of them. Persephone was so lovely and pale. Hades was grim as death. Apollo was cool and golden. He was breathtakingly handsome, but maybe a little shifty. Bridget thought fondly of her dad. He wasn't the best-looking guy in the world, but he sure did adore her mom.

Bridget felt sort of sorry for Persephone. She tiptoed even closer, trying to see the young goddess's expression. Was Persephone afraid, sad, lonely? The goddess seemed so young compared to the other Olympians, a girl not much older than Bridget, faced with the awesome choice of having to marry either the god of the Sun or the Lord of the Dead. Plus, Persephone's mom! Any mom could drive a girl crazy, but what if your mom was a real goddess? You wouldn't have a chance. And Demeter wasn't just any goddess; she was the one they called the Great Goddess, in charge of all plants. The whole world would soon starve to death if Demeter did not get her way.

Hermes stood at the edge of the group of gods and goddesses, his back to Bridget. She noticed the small leather bag that hung from his waist. It had smelled of fruit. All of a sudden,

Hades' helmet slipped down over Bridget's eyes, blocking her sight. It was a strange thing to be invisible, yet discover the helmet could slide down over your eyes and somehow block your vision. Bridget pushed up the helmet. There was that little leather bag. Now, why was it so interesting? Hmm.

The pomegranate! That was what was in Hermes' little bag. No wonder it smelled of fruit. All the stories about Persephone agreed about the pomegranate. Maybe it seemed a little weird but for some reason, if you ate any food in Hades' kingdom, you belonged to the Lord of the Dead for all time. And according to the stories, it was because Persephone ate half a dozen pomegranate seeds that she was doomed to live with Hades.

Bridget got an idea. Maybe there was still a way she could save Persephone and end winter forever. After all, she was only half a dozen feet away from Hermes. And she did have a sharp pocketknife. Very, very slowly, Bridget tiptoed toward Hermes.

Zeus said, "Let the girl talk."

"Persephone, keep quiet!" Demeter snapped. "I will speak for my daughter."

"No, we will hear from the girl. Come forward, Persephone."

Demeter grimaced angrily.

Without lifting her head, Persephone took a short step toward Zeus and Hera.

"Do you wish to leave my brother?" Zeus asked.

"Ha!" Demeter shouted. "Of course, she desires to leave him. Persephone despises Hades. All her life, she's lived amid beauty, sunshine, flowers, life! Do you think any daughter of mine can bear to live in Hades' world of gloom? It's ridiculous!"

Watching from the side of the hall, the god Ares saw a most peculiar sight. A small leather bag attached to a thong that wound around the waist of the god Hermes moved slightly; it moved by itself! The strand that tied it to the thong came apart. The bag floated in the air. As if it was a feather caught in a gust of wind, it zigzagged away from Hermes, then abruptly vanished.

The goddess Hera clapped her hands. "I have heard enough of this nonsense. All these questions about whether she wants one or the other of them are beside the point. Everyone here knows the law. Did the girl eat or drink while she stayed in Hades' kingdom? That is all that matters. If she did not, she can still be given to Apollo. If she did, then she belongs to Hades. Hermes!"

The golden god stepped forward.

"Did you do as I said?" Hera stomped her sandaled foot, gazed at the other Olympians. "I ordered Hermes to discover whether this girl drank or ate while in Hades' kingdom. Well, Hermes, what did you find? Did she eat his food or not?"

Hermes bowed to Hera. "Your Majesty, I did as you asked. Soon after I arrived in the underworld, a shade came to me. He told me that he observed Persephone pluck a pomegranate from a tree."

"Pluck it? But did she eat any of it?"

"The shade did not see her eat but swore she held the fruit in her hand. He showed me the tree."

"Did you investigate no further?"

"Among its roots, in the soft dirt, I found the footprints of Persephone. At the base of the tree, I found two halves of a pomegranate."

"Neither half was eaten?"

"At first, it seemed both halves were whole and perfect. Then, looking more closely, I discovered that one of the halves contained seeds."

"Seeds?"

"Where twelve seeds should have been, I found but six."

"Then she consumed the missing six seeds!"

"Your Majesty, here is the pomegranate. I have brought it from the Land of the Dead for your inspection." Hermes reached down to take up the small bag.

"What is it? Where is the fruit, Hermes?"

The golden god's fingers gripped the air where the bag was supposed to be. "It is gone!" Hermes caught up the cord. "Cut!"

"Cut? What do you mean? Cut how?"

"Your Majesty"—Hermes looked up at Hera, who had half-risen from her throne—"I have been robbed."

All the gods and goddesses gasped in astonishment. Who could possibly be so bold as to rob the god Hermes? And to commit theft right in the throne room of Zeus!

"Ha!" Demeter cried. "Who can believe so unlikely a story? There is no evidence. My daughter never once ate or drank while in Hades' custody. Zeus, you must rule against Hades. Give me back my stolen daughter, or else my curse remains in place, and all the world will die."

Hera sniffed loudly. "I can see no way out of this, Zeus. If there is not evidence, then you must marry the girl to Apollo, as you intended."

"Hey! Help!" A loud shriek interrupted the proceedings.

At the edge of the cluster of gods and goddesses, Ares was performing a strange dance. It was almost as if the god of War had hold of something invisible.

"Ares, how dare you interrupt us?" Hera demanded. "Quit that, whatever you are doing!"

With one hand, Ares gripped something invisible. With his other hand, he groped the air until he seized something.

Pop! Bridget suddenly became visible. Ares held her by the back of her shirt. His other hand held Hades' helmet of invisibility.

"My bag! The pomegranate!" Hermes cried.

Bridget was caught red-handed, clutching the stolen leather sack.

"We will deal with this little thief in a moment," Hera said. "Hermes, fetch the bag."

"Wait, please!" Bridget tried to talk, but Ares put his huge, calloused hand over her mouth.

"Silence!" Zeus cried. "Ares, control your prisoner. Hermes, fetch the bag."

Half-throttled by Ares, Bridget subsided. Hermes took the bag from Bridget and carried it to Zeus. The Father god opened the bag, extracted the two halves of a pomegranate. He looked at each of them carefully, then passed them to his wife Hera.

"It is as Hermes testified," Hera declared. "Six seeds are missing. The girl must remain with Hades."

Demeter cried out in anger.

"But I did not eat anything," said a small voice.

All of them turned to look at Persephone, for it was she who had spoken. "It is true that I held the fruit in my hand, but I did not consume even a single seed."

"Have you no honor?" Hera snapped. "I am the Protectress of Marriage and cannot allow our law to be violated. Persephone has eaten the food of Hades. Zeus, it is time for you to rule. Give the girl to Hades."

Persephone said nothing, but bright red spots appeared in her cheeks.

"Then all the world will die," Demeter declared bitterly.

Zeus seemed ready to rule when suddenly Hades stepped forward. "Halt!" He held up his hand. "I will not allow this miscarriage of justice. It is not Persephone who lacks honor, but me."

"You?" Zeus asked. "My brother, what have you to say?"

"It was I who sent the shade to Hermes. I saw Persephone hold the fruit in her hand, but I also saw that she did not taste its flesh, but set it on the ground at the foot of the tree. It was I who took the six seeds from its heart, not Persephone. I have them still." Hades held out his huge hand. On his palm lay the six seeds.

"Hades," Zeus asked, not unkindly, "how could you do such a thing? I was ready to rule in your favor."

"So great is my love for Persephone," said the Lord of the Dead, "I sought to keep her by any means. But I cannot hold her by so ignoble a trick."

Bridget could not help herself. Although ordered to keep silent, she murmured, "You poor guy." She'd never seen anything so tragic. Her heart went out to Hades. The poor guy was actually lovesick.

Hades turned to Persephone. "You are free to go to Apollo. I give up any claim I have to you." He turned to Apollo and bowed.

"No," said a soft voice.

It was Persephone. The pale and beautiful goddess took a step toward Hades. She touched his fist until he opened it to reveal the half dozen seeds. One by one, before all the Olympians, Persephone consumed each of the seeds. In this way, she took Hades as her lawful husband.

Afterward, back in the anteroom, Bridget told the others, "I just about cried. I tell you, it was the most romantic thing I ever saw in my life. She loves the big guy."

Babette, Beauregard, and Barnaby agreed it was definitely a surprise ending to the story of Persephone and Hades, but they were terribly worried about what was going to happen to Bridget. After all, she had "borrowed" Hades' helmet of invisibility. Worse, Bridget had trespassed on the secret deliberations of the Olympians. She had stolen Hermes' little sack and concealed evidence in an important hearing.

Zeus had ordered that Bridget be returned to her friends. He would decide her punishment after he finished ruling on the dispute between Demeter and Hades. Ares had carried Bridget back here to the anteroom.

Barnaby, Babette, and Beauregard exchanged worried looks. Bridget was acting pretty cool, but who knew what terrible fate might be in store for her? Maybe she'd wind up in Tartarus with the other people who had dared to commit crimes against the gods. For all they knew, she might be sentenced to push a big rock up a hill for all eternity, or stand in that pond beside the guy who never got to eat or drink.

The door to the anteroom swung open. Hermes looked at all of them. He looked very grave. "All of you are to come with me. Zeus will see you now."

Chapter 15
Olympian Laughter

Hermes marched the group to the throne room of Zeus, where the Father God would judge them. Hermes walked them a little too fast, and he did not allow any talking. What had happened to the charming young god they had met in the underworld? Now, Hermes was all business. It was like being marched to the principal's office, except worse. Lots worse.

Bridget was trying to look brave, but it was obvious she was worried. Barnaby and Babette were worried too. Everyone knew how seriously the gods took any insult. Bridget had actually crept into Zeus's throne room and stolen something from Hermes. No wonder the messenger of Zeus no longer smiled at them.

Even if we are not punished, Barnaby thought, how are we ever going to get back to New York City?

Hermes threw open the doors to the great hall. Zeus sat all by himself on his golden throne. A nimbus of light surrounded him as if he was enveloped in static electricity. Zeus was the god of thunder. He did not look happy.

Hermes marched them to the foot of Zeus's throne. Up close, the chief of all the gods was enormous, at least eight feet tall and four hundred pounds. Barnaby thought, He's bigger than Shaquille O'Neill!

The field of electromagnetism around Zeus was so powerful it made Beauregard's hair stand on end. It made Barnaby's hair even bushier and more bristly than ever.

"Halt!" commanded Hermes. "Here are the prisoners, mighty Zeus."

"Prisoners!" Bridget yelped. "Who are you calling—"

"Silence!" thundered Zeus. Outside his palace, lightning cracked.

The kids and Beauregard jumped as if a cannon had just been fired inches from their heads.

"Hermes," Zeus commanded, "read the charges against these puny criminals who have dared invade Olympus and disturb the peace of the gods."

Criminals! thought Bridget. And who's he calling puny? But she had sense enough to keep her mouth shut.

Hermes read the charges against them. "You are accused of the following crimes: One, violation of your oaths to Aphrodite and Hermes. Two, theft of Hephaestus's golden horse and a golden head. Also, theft of Hades' helmet of invisibility. Also, theft of Hermes' property. Three, abuse of the hospitality of Almighty Zeus. Four, trespass upon the holy places, first Hades' kingdom, second the throne room of Zeus. Fifth, hubris, the crime of pride and arrogance." Hermes looked up at Zeus. "That concludes the list of their crimes, mighty Zeus. How do you judge them?"

"Hold on!" Bridget yelled. She was so mad her face had turned red. "How can he judge us when we haven't even had a chance to defend ourselves? What kind of court is this?"

"Let the criminal speak," Zeus said. Above the palace, lightning cracked again, this time so loudly the entire building shook.

"There you go again. Criminal. How can you call me a criminal when you haven't even heard my side of it? I thought you were supposed to be an impartial judge!" Bridget was not the daughter of a good lawyer for nothing.

"Let the mortal speak," Zeus said. Lightning cracked again; thunder rolled through the palace.

"Be careful, Bridget," Barnaby whispered.

Bridget took a deep breath. "First of all, we never violated our oaths. We promised Aphrodite not to tell Demeter that Hades was going to kidnap Persephone, and we never did tell her. We never even got to her island until after Hades took Persephone, so how could we have violated our oath to Aphrodite? And our oath to Hermes, if you mean to stay back there in the waiting room, the others promised Hermes that, but I never did. And they did stay back there, so they never violated their oath to Hermes either."

Bridget stopped to get her breath, then went on. "As for those theft charges, Hephaestus lent us the golden horse. He gave us the golden head to be our guide. If he wants her back, all he has to do is visit the Pythoness in Delphi. As for Hades' helmet, I just borrowed it. I wasn't gonna keep it. And that bag, well, okay, maybe I did steal it, but it was just to save Persephone. I think eating some seeds is a silly reason to make someone get married anyway. And how was I to know she really, truly loved him?"

"Have you no more to say in your defense, little mortal?"

"Well, gimme a second to think. You say we're guilty of abuse of hospitality and of trespass. Well, you can't have it both ways. We were invited here by Hermes. He said you wanted to see us. He brought us here. So how did we trespass if we were invited?"

"The final charge," Zeus said, "is hubris, the crime of arrogance and pride. How do you answer that charge, little one?"

Bridget hung her head. "Well, maybe I do get carried away with myself sometimes." The back of her neck felt hot. "I thought I was doing the right thing anyway." She looked up at Zeus. "Aw, please, mighty Zeus, they say you are always on the side of justice. You can do what you like to me, but you gotta let my friends go. They're innocent!"

"Have you finished? None of you has anything further to say?"

Barnaby, Babette, and Beauregard stepped forward. "Wait!"

A crack of thunder froze them in their places. Barnaby swallowed loudly.

"Speak!" thundered Zeus.

"Go on, Barnaby," Babette said.

"Yes," Beauregard said, "Barnaby speaks for all of us."

"Bridget is truly sorry for what she did," Barnaby said. "She didn't know any better. It's like she said. Everything she did was done in a good cause. At least, she thought it was a good cause. It's just she's a little impulsive. Really, she's a great person once you get to know her."

"That is right, Monsieur Zeus," Babette said.

"Exactly!" Beauregard lashed his tail. "Brave as a lion."

"In any case, mighty Zeus," Barnaby said, "we are all in this together. If you punish Bridget, we want you to punish us too."

"Yes, Monsieur Zeus," agreed Babette. "If Bridget did anything wrong, we are equally guilty."

"One for all, and all for one," Beauregard said. He wiggled his whiskers and tried to look as innocent as possible considering he was a cat.

Zeus looked hard at all of them. His face turned dark. It was an enormous face that somehow resembled an approaching storm. Electricity snapped all around him as if he was about to start shooting off sparks.

The kids stepped backward. They huddled together, putting their arms around one another. All of them remembered those stories in which Zeus knocked someone dead by hurling a thunderbolt at him.

"Please, sir," Bridget whispered.

Zeus slapped his knees with both hands. He heaved back in his throne, threw back his head, and roared.

The kids jumped. They looked at Zeus in astonishment.

Zeus laughed so hard he shook the palace. He slapped his knees and stomped his feet. Hermes laughed too. He could not help himself. Zeus's Olympian laughter was contagious. Pretty soon, Bridget snickered. Barnaby chuckled. Babette laughed out loud. They didn't even know why they were laughing. They fell against one another, laughing so hard their sides hurt.

Olympian laughter is even better than normal human laughter. Olympian laughter makes the sun come out. When Zeus laughs, he causes birds to sing and plants to grow. He heals the sick and cheers up the dead.

Zeus laughed and laughed until the kids and Beauregard did not have a care in the world. He laughed until the whole universe felt good about itself. Finally, he wheezed to a stop and wiped away his tears.

"If there's one thing I admire," he smiled at them, "it's courage. I'll say that for you. You don't give up. And you stick together. I admire that too."

"Shall I call for Hephaestus, mighty Zeus?" Hermes asked.

"Yes, go ahead. Bring him in here, and bring in that contraption he's made, that cabinet."

Hermes vanished quick as thought.

"I've been watching you ever since you appeared in the Swamps of Lerna," Zeus said. "I know you didn't really steal Hephaestus' horse or the golden head either. And I know you kept your oaths to Aphrodite and Hermes. And you, little thief," he pointed to Bridget, "I know you have a good heart even if you haven't much common sense." He smiled forgivingly and wiped away another tear. "I hope you will forgive me my little joke, but even we Olympians like to have fun now and then." He motioned them to come closer to him. "I've decided to spare your lives, even yours, little thief!" He winked at Bridget. "When you stole that bag from Hermes! Funniest thing I ever saw! The expression on his face when he found it gone!" Zeus roared.

When he got control of himself, Zeus continued, "Where you went wrong was thinking you could change fate, save Persephone and end winter. Now, what would Old Man Winter do if he couldn't paint frost on your windows and hang icicles from your eaves? And doesn't my brother Hades need a loving spouse, like anyone else? No, I'm not going to punish you, not even you, little thief. But I am sending you home before you get into more trouble!" He looked up. "Hephaestus! Bring that in here."

The doors to the throne room swung open. Hermes entered. A huge wooden box the size of a telephone booth followed him. Its sides were covered with carvings.

"It's the Cabinet of Hephaestus!" Barnaby cried.

Hephaestus himself followed the cabinet right into the middle of the throne room. His invention was self propelled. It rolled obediently in front of him.

"Hello, Beauregard," said a familiar voice.

"Branwell!" Beauregard said.

On top of the cabinet sat Beauregard's cousin, Branwell.

"I brought him along," Hephaestus smiled. "He was getting a little tired of Aphrodite's temple."

Zeus leapt down from his throne to inspect the cabinet. Like all the gods, he took enormous pleasure in all the works of Hephaestus, the artist and craftsman of the gods. "Beautiful workmanship!" Zeus bent over the carvings, the scenes of the gods and goddesses. "Why, here's Heracles. And isn't this one Persephone?" At Zeus's touch, the doors to the cabinet swung open. "And it works perfectly, does it?"

Hephaestus nodded. "My inventions always work," he said mildly. "Once they enter the cabinet, and we close the doors, they will be returned to their world."

"Oh, yes, their world, the other world. It must be awfully dull, eh?" Zeus looked at all of them. "I feel quite sorry for you. Of course, you would rather stay here, but there is no help for it. We can't have you getting into trouble day and night. It is my wish that all of you go at once. Good-bye, good-bye." Zeus motioned them into the cabinet.

Beauregard and Branwell led the way.

"Good-bye!" Hermes called.

"Farewell," said Hephaestus.

Babette, Bridget, and Barnaby followed the cats. The cabinet was a tight fit. When all five of them were inside it, they were wedged together so tightly they could not move.

"Good-bye!" they yelled. "Thank you! Thanks for every-thing!"

"Oh, dear," Zeus said. "Hermes, haven't we forgotten someone?"

Hermes nodded. "The pig, your Majesty."

"Oh, yes. Well, go fetch him." As Hermes vanished, Zeus smiled graciously at the kids. "A brief delay. Comfortable?"

"We're fine, sir," Barnaby lied. "Couldn't be more com-fortable." Bridget was standing on his toe. Beauregard's ear tickled his chin. And someone else, perhaps Babette, was breathing onto the back of his neck.

"Here we are," Zeus said.

The door of the throne room flew open. Carrying a large bag, Hermes entered. The bag was lumpy. It wriggled.

"Perhaps," said Beauregard, "we should exit the cabinet just to see what is in the bag?"

"Yes, indeed," agreed Zeus. "Come right out. You must see this."

"Yipes!" yelled Bridget. Someone had just poked her in a sensitive spot.

The kids spilled out of the cabinet all at once, sprawling every which way.

"Everyone all right?" Zeus asked.

Bridget picked herself up off the floor. "You think he's gonna make us take what's in the bag? There's not enough room in the cabinet as it is."

"Pour him out, by all means," commanded Zeus. "Let's have a look at him."

Hermes untied the bag and upended it. Out fell a fat pink pig. The porker hit the floor with its rump and squealed like—well, like a pig. It was a very big pig, as heavy as a man.

"Hold onto one of his hind legs," Zeus told Hermes. "We don't want him running around loose."

Hermes obediently gripped the pig's left hind leg, causing it to squeal loudly.

"I believe this pig belongs to you," Zeus said.

"To us, sir?" asked Barnaby.

"Is he one of their servants, Hermes?"

Hermes murmured something that only Zeus could hear.

"I see," the father god said. "Well, they must know him."

"We've never seen this pig before," Babette said. "At least, I do not think so."

"I'm sure we'd remember him if we had seen him," Beauregard added. "He's such a homely fellow." And indeed the pig was homely, even for a pig. He was so pink, so free of hair, that he resembled the top of a bald man's head.

"I don't get it," Bridget said. "But he does look sort of familiar."

"This pig," Zeus said, "is a magician, a rather st magician, I am afraid. He came from your world, not after you," Zeus pointed at Beauregard's cousin, Branwell.

"After me, sir?" Branwell asked.

"Like you, he visited Aphrodite's palace. He snuck in, I am told."

Branwell gazed in astonishment at the pig. "He did?" He looked up quickly. "Not that I doubt you for a moment, your Majesty. I just don't recall seeing him, or any other pig for that matter, while I stayed with the lovely goddess." Branwell remembered several magnificent peacocks but not a single pig.

"Have you obtained the magician's box, Hermes?"

"Here it is, your Majesty," Hermes produced a small object, which he handed to Zeus.

"This fellow was not always a wretched pig. Until he offended the goddess Aphrodite, he was human."

"Human? Him?" Barnaby stared at the pig, who seemed to be 100 percent pig from his curly tail to his round pink snout.

"Upon entering Aphrodite's palace, the silly fellow attempted to entrap the goddess."

"Entrap her!" Branwell exclaimed. "Entrap Aphrodite? How could he possibly—?"

"I must admit I do not quite understand the method, some sort of enchantment. He failed, of course, but not before he managed to capture a little bit of the goddess. Fortunately, Aphrodite discovered him and, well, you see how she punished him."

"My goodness," Babette said. "A bit of her? What bit?"

Zeus turned briskly. "Hermes, show them the—what is it?"

Hermes produced a small flat object. For a moment, the kids supposed it was a picture postcard.

"Your Majesty?" Beauregard asked. "Could we see the magician's little box?"

Zeus held it out. All of them stared. Their mouths fell open. There, in the middle of Zeus's large hand, was a camera. The "picture postcard" in his other hand was in fact a photograph.

"It's a Polaroid!" exclaimed Barnaby. On the photo was a blurry image of the gorgeous Aphrodite taking a bath.

Beauregard rumbled. "I believe," he swished his tail angrily, "I have solved the mystery of the pig's identity."

"Good!" Zeus beamed. "We hoped you would."

"The magician," Beauregard stood on his hind legs, "was he portly, sir?"

"Yes, indeed."

Zeus murmured agreement.

"Wore a horizontally striped shirt, did he?"

Zeus said, "Absolutely."

Babette, Barnaby, and Bridget stared at the pig.

"It can't be!" said Bridget.

"I will reverse the spell," Zeus declared. He snapped his fingers.

Hermes released the pig's hind leg. As if an invisible hammer had smacked it on the cranium, the animal slumped to the floor. Its eyes closed.

"Wow, look at that," Bridget murmured.

The pig's hind legs began to grow. The cloven hooves sprouted toes, human toes. Then, the pig's front legs grew long, sprouted fingers—chubby human fingers. Clothing appeared on the pig. Dirty sneakers. Dirty blue jeans. A striped tee shirt. The pig's head was the last part of it to transform. It bulged here; it shrunk there. It altered in any number of ways until at last, on the floor at their feet, was someone they recognized, a fat, bald man.

"Cue Ball!" yelled Bridget.

It was indeed Merlin "Cue Ball" Ozymandias, the owner of the curio shop in New York's Greenwich Village, the man who had taken Bridget's prized baseball, the home run ball hit by Reggie Jackson, in exchange for allowing them to try out the Cabinet of Hephaestus.

The bald man's eyes popped open. "Hey, who's calling me Cue Ball?"

"If I were you, Merlin," Beauregard said. "I would not give any more offense."

Cue Ball sighed and stood up slowly, shaking out his sore limbs. He noticed the god Hephaestus standing near the cabinet. He took a peek at Hermes, who was frowning as if thinking of again transforming Cue Ball into a pig. He saw the mighty Zeus and dropped to his knees. "Pardon! Pardon me!"

"Well, go ahead, little man," Zeus commanded, "explain yourself. How dare you trespass upon the goddess Aphrodite's privacy? How dare you try to entrap her in your magic box?"

In the next few minutes, Cue Ball confessed how he'd been led to the misstep. Back in New York, after Beauregard and the kids had disappeared into the cabinet, a customer had entered his shop. It had taken Cue Ball several minutes to get rid of the customer. While he'd waited on the customer, he'd had the most intense sensation that someone else had run into his store, not a person exactly, perhaps a dog?

"Not a dog but a cat. Must have been Branwell," Beauregard said, swishing his tail. "He arrived a little late. Followed us, you know."

"You see"—Cue Ball's eyes lit up—"all my life I studied mythology. And here was a chance to see it, actually observe it with my own eyes. The Land of Myth! Can you blame a guy for wanting to see it? How could I pass up the chance?" He looked up at Zeus. "I couldn't help myself. I meant no harm, your Mightiness. I got my camera and entered the cabinet. I ended up at a palace, see, not just any palace, Aphrodite's Palace! Most beautiful place I ever saw in my life!" Cue Ball bit his lip. "I only took one picture. It ain't even that good of a picture. You can only see her back."

Beauregard explained to Zeus that Cue Ball had not exactly stolen a "little bit" of Aphrodite, nor had he tried to "entrap" the goddess in his camera. "All the little box is, well, it's a sort of machine that makes pictures of things. It's not magical at all. It's what we call a camera, a Polaroid camera."

"Hmm." Zeus peered at the photo. "If I destroy this image, I will not harm Aphrodite?"

"Not at all, your Highness."

Zeus opened his hand. As if it were a tiny flying carpet, the photo of Aphrodite floated into the air, drifted here and there, until it came to a burning torch. The photo hesitated a moment, then dove into the heart of the flame. It darkened, burst into flames. The ashes snowed to the floor.

"Oh, thank you, Father Zeus," Cue Ball cried. "Thank you for not sentencing me to death!"

"Good-bye all," Zeus smiled. "And you"—the father god pointed directly at Cue Ball—"keep in mind you have offended a goddess. Although I will pardon you this time, I advise you never again to return to this world. Do you understand?"

"Oh, my, you bet, sir! Thank you. Never again will I come back, never! I swear!"

"Hermes, see that all of them get home safely, will you?" Zeus swept out of the throne room, moving as grandly as if he were a battleship leaving a harbor.

All of them, Barnaby, Babette, Bridget, Cue Ball, Beauregard, and Branwell, squeezed themselves into the cabinet. With the plump Cue Ball included, it was an even tighter fit than before.

"I feel like a sardine!" Bridget grumbled. All by itself, the cabinet door swung shut. They were plunged into darkness. The cabinet began to move, to shake. It slid forward and back.

Bang!

"What happened?" Babette whispered.

Dead silence.

"Everybody all right?" Beauregard called. "Anyone hurt?"

"Open the door!" yelled Bridget. "I can hardly breathe in here."

The cabinet's door flew open. For a moment, none of them could move, then someone yelped, and all of them burst out of the cabinet, landing in a big pile.

"Where are we?" Barnaby yelled.

They rolled apart, looked around. They were in the back room of Cue Ball's curio shop.

Cue Ball squinted at a clock on the wall. "Hmm," he said, pointing, "ain't much time passed."

"But is it the same day?" Beauregard asked. Was it possible? They'd been shut up in the cabinet for only sixteen minutes?

Cue Ball shot a serious glare at Bridget. "Don't think for a second I'm giving back your home run ball."

"A quarter hour!" Bridget yelped. She could hardly believe it. They could all get back to her apartment as if nothing had happened. She'd been scared to death her parents would have called the police by now.

"Now, get outta my store," Cue Ball ordered. "I've had enough of all of you. You heard me. I'm closing up! Go on. Scram!"

It seemed miraculous. Perhaps Barnaby's theory of "mythic time" was right after all. They'd bounced around the mythical world for days, but in this world, the real one, they'd been gone only a few minutes.

all I know is," Bridget said, "it's good to be home."

led them out of the store, followed by Barnaby, and the two cats.

Outside Cue Ball's shop, snow was falling. It was late afternoon, almost dark. Despite their amazing adventure, it seemed as if life in New York City was going on pretty much as normal. The streetlights were winking on. Fat, white flakes zigzagged down through the air. Bridget stuck out her tongue and caught one.

As they trudged home, they passed Rockefeller Center, a tall building that goes up and up as if it wants to touch the sky. At its base, in the wintertime, is a skating rink.

It was completely dark now, and spotlights caused the skating rink to gleam like the moon. The skaters, all bundled up, went around and around the radiant circle. The sky-scrapers all around looked on majestically. Maybe winter wasn't so unbearable after all. The kids all seemed lost in their own thoughts. It seemed weird to return from so far away, to have seen so many amazing sights, then return here to the ordinary world. It was almost as if they had never left. It was good to be back, but in a way, they all felt a little sad.

Above the skating rink was a statue, an enormous golden statue, not of a Greek god, but of a Titan. The ancient Greeks believed that, before the gods came, the earth was ruled by a race of giants called the Titans. The gigantic golden statue was an image of the Titan called Prometheus. He had given fire to humankind. For doing so, the gods had punished him terribly. But the name of the statue was "Prometheus Unbound." The golden giant seemed to fly through the air, free as a bird.

"In a way, the gods are gone," Babette said. "At least it seems like it. They are forgotten now, and no one worships them. No one builds temples for them any more. Yet, in lots of ways, we remember them." She turned to Barnaby.

"Are you glad we went to the Land of Myth, Barnaby?"

"Oh, yes," Barnaby said.

"What a great adventure we had," Bridget sighed.

Beauregard purred contentedly.

The skaters whirled around and around the ice rink. The snow fell and, for a time, the world seemed hushed and splendid.

Glossary

Actaeon (AK-tee-uhn)
Actaeon was a hunter who innocently surprised Artemis bathing naked in the woods. Angered at the violation of her privacy, the goddess changed him into a stag, and his dogs killed him.

Ambrosia (am-BROH-zhuh)
Ambrosia was the food of the gods. It preserved their immortality and conferred the qualities of divinity—beauty and strength. The drink of the gods was called nectar.

Aphrodite (af-roh-DY-tee)
Aphrodite was the goddess of love. She was said to be irresistibly beautiful, especially when she wore her magical girdle (a sort of sash). She was known to the Romans as Venus. Aphrodite is sometimes described as the daughter of Zeus and Dione; other sources declare that she was born from the foam of the sea. She had many lovers, including the war-god Ares. She was the wife of Hephaestus and the mother of Eros.

Apollo (a-POLL-oh)
Apollo and his twin sister, Artemis, were the children of Zeus and Leto. Since they were born on the island of Delos, Apollo was often called the Delian god. He was also identified with the city of Delphi, where he killed the giant serpent Python and founded the most famous center for prophecy

in the ancient world, the shrine of the Delphic Oracle. Apollo was associated with prophecy, medicine, the fine arts, archery, beauty, flocks and herds, law, courage, and wisdom. He became, next to Zeus, the god most revered by the Greeks and is often said to be the god who best embodied the Greek spirit. He is also considered the sun god, though others associate this role with the god Helios.

Athena (a-THEEN-uh)

Athena was the goddess of wisdom; she is especially associated with the city of Athens. She was a virgin goddess.

Ares (AIR-eez)

Ares, the son of Zeus, was the god of war, the god who loves battle and bloodshed. He was never especially popular with the Greeks but turned to in time of war. Ares was loved by Aphrodite; they produced several children. In Roman mythology, he was called Mars.

Artemis (AHR-tuh-mis)

Artemis was goddess of the hunt. She was the mistress of wild things and the protector of women. In contrast to the sexy Aphrodite, Artemis was associated with chaste love. She is usually depicted as lean and athletic and is frequently accompanied by a deer. She was the twin sister of Apollo and the daughter of Zeus and Leto. Artemis was also identified with the Moon, though some associate the moon with the goddess Selene. To the Romans, Artemis was Diana.

Centaur (SEN-tar)

A centaur was half man and half horse. Centaurs were men from head to waist. Most of them were crude and savage, but some were well educated and talented.

Daedalus (DED-uh-luhs)

Daedalus was a mortal, but a great architect and inventor. Credited with many inventions, he built a Labyrinth to house the Minotaur for King Minos. When Minos imprisoned him,

Daedalus escaped with his son, Icarus, on wings of waxed feathers. Icarus flew too close to the sun. As a result, his wings melted, and he fell into the sea.

Delphi (DEL-fy)
Delphi, located on the lower southern slopes of Mount Parnassus near the Gulf of Corinth, was a sacred city to the ancient Greeks. It was called the omphalos (navel or center) of the Earth, and this was designated by a large, rounded, conical stone, which was also called the omphalos. Delphi was sacred to Apollo, whose famous temple and prophetic shrine were there. The temple within the surrounding sanctuary was the home of the famous

Delphic Oracle
Delphi was also sacred to Dionysius, the god associated with wine, fertility, and wild dancing. In honor of the killing of the monster Python by Apollo, the Pythian Games were held in Delphi every four years.

Demeter (dih-MEE-tur)
Demeter was the goddess of plants and agriculture. She was the mother of Persephone. When Persephone was abducted by Hades, god of the dead, Demeter cursed the Earth's crops; nothing could grow. Starvation threatened the world until Zeus ruled that Persephone spent six months with Hades (autumn and winter) and six months with her mother (spring and summer). Demeter's joy at Persephone's return caused the barren earth to blossom each year. In Roman mythology, Demeter was called Ceres.

Dionysius (dy-uh-NY-suhs)
Dionysius was the ancient god of fertility, ritual dance, and mysticism. He invented wine making and was considered the patron of poetry, song, and drama. In many ways, he seems the opposite type of Apollo. They represent the two sides of creativity: the wild and original side, and the balanced, order-making aspect.

Eros (AIR-ohz)

Eros was the son of Aphrodite. He was the god of sudden, violent love. He was frequently depicted as causing love by shooting arrows into people who would then find themselves hopelessly in love with someone else. Many of his antics are related in the Metamorphoses of Ovid. He is usually depicted with wings, carrying a bow and wearing a quiver of arrows. In Roman mythology he is called Cupid or Amor.

Hades (HAY-deez)

Hades was the god of the underworld. He ruled over the souls of the dead with the aid of his wife, Persephone. Hades also became known as the underworld itself—the world of the dead, separated from the world of the living by the River Styx and its tributaries, the Acheron, Lethe, Cocytus, and Phlegethon. New arrivals to the Land of the Dead were ferried across the Styx by Charon. Trespassers who dared to enter Hades uninvited could expect to be confronted by the three-headed dog, Cerberus. The three judges of the dead decided where a soul would go. The virtuous went to Elysium (also known as the Elysian Fields). The wicked went to Tartarus, a place of punishment. Those who were neither especially good or especially wicked went to Asphodel Meadows. The Romans called the god of the dead Pluto.

Hephaestus (huh-FES-tuhs)

Hephaestus was the god of fire and the patron of craftsmen. He was always represented as lame. In some accounts, he is also described as ugly. He is the only one of the gods to be physically imperfect. Homer's Iliad includes two different accounts of his lameness. According to one story, Zeus flung him down from Olympus to the island of Lemnos for siding with Hera in a quarrel. According to the other, Hephaestus was born lame, and Hera, disgusted by his lameness, flung him from Olympus. A supreme artist and craftsman, Hephaestus made the palaces of the gods, as well as many of their weapons and possessions. In Roman mythology, Hephaestus is called Vulcan.

Hera (HAIR-uh)

Hera was the wife of Zeus and the queen of the gods. She was worshipped as the goddess of marriage, women, and childbirth. Hera's marriage to Zeus, king of the gods, was troubled by his many infidelities. Hera often persecuted the women that Zeus pursued and their offspring. In Roman mythology, Hera is called Juno.

Heracles (HAIR-uh-kleez)

Heracles is also known as Hercules. He was famous for his courage and superhuman strength. His father was the god Zeus, his mother the mortal Alcmene. He is said to have saved the gods in their war with the Titans. In Greek mythology, Heracles was the only man to make the full transition from mortal to immortal. He was eventually worshipped as a god, becoming one of the most popular gods in the ancient world. The most famous feats of Heracles are called the Twelve Labors. Different sources list them in different orders. (1) Killing the Nemean lion, which could not be killed by metal or stone; from the lion he made the cloak and club that became his trademarks; (2) killing the nine-headed Hydra, which could grow two new heads for each one it lost; the blood of the Hydra was the source of poison for Heracles' arrows, which could cause death even from a scratch; (3) capturing the golden-horned hind of Ceryneia, which was sacred to Artemis; (4) capturing the Erymanthian boar; (5) cleaning the stables of Augeas; (6) routing the Stymphalian birds, which had iron feathers and were sacred to Ares; (7) capturing the Cretan bull; (8) capturing the man-eating mares of Diomedes; (9) obtaining the girdle of Hippolyte, queen of the Amazons; (10) driving the cattle of Geryon from far west to Greece; (11) capturing Cerberus, the watchdog of the underworld; and (12) obtaining the golden apples of the Hesperides.

Hermes (HUR-meez)
Although mainly famous for his role as Zeus's messenger, Hermes was a god with many other functions: protector of flocks and shepherds; guide and protector of travelers; conductor of souls to the underworld; bringer of good luck; and patron of orators, writers, athletes, merchants, and thieves. Known for his cleverness, charm and speed, he was usually pictured with a broad-rimmed hat with wings on it, a herald's staff, winged sandals, and a shepherd's staff. The Romans called him Mercury.

Homer (HOH-mur)
Homer was the author of the epic poems *The Iliad* and *The Odyssey*. Some modern scholars believe these poems to have been written by several authors, but the ancient Greeks believed that a blind poet named Homer composed them. They are two of the most popular sources of stories about the gods and goddesses.

Hydra (HY-druh)
The Hydra was a nine-headed monster, a water serpent that lived in the Swamps of Lerna, near Argos. If one of its heads was cut off, it grew two more. The Hydra was killed by Heracles, who burned off the heads and used its blood to make poisoned arrows. The middle head of the Hydra was immortal; Heracles cut it off and hid it beneath an enormous boulder.

Minotaur (MIN-uh-tohr)
A monster, half man and half bull. Kept in the Labyrinth, a maze designed by Daedalus, where young men were annually sacrificed to him by Minos, the Minotaur was finally killed by the hero Theseus.

Nereus (NEE-ree-uhs)
Nereus was a sea god who was also known as the Old Man of the Sea. He and the Oceanid Doris were the parents of the fifty sea nymphs known as the Nereids.

Olympus, Mount (oh-LIM-pus)
Mount Olympus is the highest peak in Greece. The snowcapped mountain rises in the Olympus range in northern Greece near the Aegean coast. The cloud-covered mountain was the home of the gods.

Ovid's Metamorphoses (AH-vidz met-uh-MOHR-fuh-seez)
The Metamorphoses, the poet Ovid's masterpiece, is a Latin poem in fifteen books that describes a series of transformations. In most of these stories, humans are transformed into animals, plants, or rivers. Like Homer's epic poems, the Metamorphoses is a great source of stories about Greek mythology.

Pandora (pan-DOHR-uh)
Pandora was the first woman on Earth. She is reminiscent of Eve. Pandora was created by Hephaestus for Zeus who wanted to punish us for accepting the gift of fire that Prometheus stole from heaven. Zeus gave Pandora a box containing all the troubles that the world now knows. She was warned not to open the box, but her curiosity overcame her. Only Hope remained inside the box.

Pegasus (PEG-uh-suhs)
Pegasus was the winged horse of the Muses, born of the blood of the Medusa.

Persephone (pur-SEF-uh-nee)
Persephone (also called Kore) was the beautiful daughter of Zeus and Demeter. Hades, god of the underworld and brother of Zeus, fell in love with her. As Persephone was picking flowers one day, Hades came out of the earth and carried her off to be his queen. While the grief-stricken Demeter

searched for her daughter, the earth began to turn into a barren desert. Zeus finally ordered Persephone's release, but because she had eaten a half dozen pomegranate seeds while she was still in the underworld, she was obliged to spend half of each year there (autumn and winter). When Persephone returns to her mother, spring begins. In Roman mythology, she was called Proserpina.

Plato (PLAY-toh)
Some experts say that Plato is the most important philosopher ever. His work discussed most of the important problems and concepts of Western ethics, psychology, logic, and politics.

Poseidon (poh-SY-dun)
Poseidon was the god of the sea and of earthquakes. The brother of Zeus, he was a violent and powerful god. His chief weapon was the trident, a three-pronged spear.

Satyr (SAY-tur)
Satyrs were immortal creatures of the woods. They had the head, arms, and upper body of a man and the horns, ears, and hind legs of a goat. Satyrs loved to frolic, drink, chase nymphs, and play reed instruments. As modern kids might say, they loved to party.

Sophocles (SAHF-uh-kleez)
Sophocles was one of the greatest playwrights of the ancient world. According to tradition, he wrote 123 plays but only seven of his tragedies still survive today.

Tiresias (ty-REE-see-uhs)
Tiresias was a blind fortune teller or seer. The goddess Athena blinded him when he accidentally came upon her while she was bathing. Repenting later, the goddess made up for her cruelty by gifting him with the power of prophecy. He remained blind, however.

Zeus (zoos)

Zeus is often called the father god. He was the ruler of heaven and Earth and of all gods and humankind. Although Zeus was married to his sister Hera, he had many affairs with mortal women as well as goddesses, and he fathered many children. He was the brother of Hades and Poseidon. Zeus's weapon was the terrible thunderbolt. Zeus is also associated with divine justice. The Romans called him Jupiter.

About the Author

Dr. Gary Arms is an assistant professor in the English department of one of the Midwest's finest small colleges, Clarke College, in Dubuque, Iowa. He lives in a comfortable old house with his beautiful wife, Susie, and Joe and David, the Wonder Boys.

Notes:

Notes:

Notes:

Notes:

Notes:

More Bestselling Smart Junior Titles from The Princeton Review

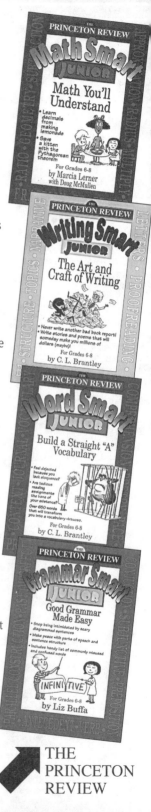

A 1995 Parents Choice Gold Medal Award-Winning Series

Join Barnaby, Babette, Bridget, their fat cat friend Beauregard, and all the crazy people they meet as they travel around the world, across time, and through space in search of adventure and knowledge.

"Educational and entertaining describes this series. The Princeton Review has made learning just plain fun."
—*Writing Teacher* magazine

AMERICAN HISTORY SMART JUNIOR
$12.00 • 0-679-77357-6
A time travel adventure through history!

ASTRONOMY SMART JUNIOR
$12.00 • 0-679-76906-4
Blast off to Mars with the Smart Junior gang.

GEOGRAPHY SMART JUNIOR
$12.00 • 0-679-77522-6
The Smart Junior gang has to solve a mystery by finding clues from all over the world.

GRAMMAR SMART JUNIOR
$12.00 • 0-679-76212-4
Good grammar made easy. Selected by *Curriculum Administrator* magazine readers as one of the Top 100 Products of 1995-96.

MATH SMART JUNIOR
$12.00 • 0-679-75935-2
Save a kitten with the Pythagorean theorem and more! "Learning at its giggliest," says the *Chicago Tribune KIDNEWS.*

WORD SMART JUNIOR
$12.00 • 0-679-75936-0
Build a straight A vocabulary with the Smart Junior gang as they have a crazy adventure with over 650 vocabulary words.

WRITING SMART JUNIOR
$12.00 • 0-679-76131-4
Book reports, school papers, letter writing, story writing and even poetry are covered in *Writing Smart Junior,* selected by The New York Public Library for its 1996 Books for the Teen Age List.

THE
PRINCETON
REVIEW